"The Communists, therefore, are on the one hand, practically the most advanced and resolute section of the working-class parties of every country, that section which pushes forward all others; on the other hand, theoretically, they have over the great mass of the proletariat the advantage of clearly understanding the line of march, the conditions, and the ultimate general results of the proletarian movement."
Marx and Engels, *The Communist Manifesto*,1848.

GH00984789

LINE OF MARCH

A Historical and Critical Analysis of British Communism and its Revolutionary Strategy

MAX ADERETH

Preface and Postscript by Ron Bellamy

PRAXIS PRESS 2020

FIRST PUBLISHED IN 1994, REPUBLISHED TO CELEBRATE THE CENTENARY OF THE
COMMUNIST PARTY IN BRITAIN 1920-2020

LINE OF MARCH

A Historical and Critical Analysis of British Communism and its Revolutionary Strategy

MAX ADERETH

Preface and Postscript
by Ron Bellamy

ISBN-13 978-1-899155-10-1
EAN 9781899155101

Published by Praxis Press
Email: praxispress@me.com
Website: redletterspp.com

Praxis Press:

c/o Unity Books,
72 Waterloo Street,
Glasgow, G2 7DA,
Scotland, Great Britain
T: +44 141 204 1611
E: enquiries@unitybooks.co.uk
www.unitybooks.co.uk

CONTENTS

Abbreviations

CP   Communist Party
        (a) Party programmes
        The British Road to Socialism (1951, 1952, 1958, 1968, 1978,
        1989/91)
        BRS Britain's Road to Socialism   (2000, 2011, 2018)
        DP   Draft Programme (1939)
        FSB   For Soviet Britain (1935)
CPB   Communist Party of Britain
CPC   Communist Party of China
CPCz   Communist Party of Czechoslovakia
CPGB   Communist Party of Great Britain
CPSU   Communist Party of the Soviet Union
PCE   Spanish Communist Party
PCI   Italian Communist Party
EC   Executive Committee
LP   Labour Party
LSI   Labour and Socialist International, also known as the
        Second International
TUC   Trades Union Congress
USSR   Union of Soviet Socialist Republics, also known as the Soviet Union

CONTENTS

Abbreviations

CP   Communist Party
(a) Party programmes
The British Road to Socialism (1951, 1952, 1958, 1968, 1978, 1989/91)
BRS Britain's Road to Socialism   (2000, 2011, 2018)
DP   Draft Programme (1939)
FSB   For Soviet Britain (1935)

CPB	Communist Party of Britain
CPC	Communist Party of China
CPCz	Communist Party of Czechoslovakia
CPGB	Communist Party of Great Britain
CPSU	Communist Party of the Soviet Union
PCE	Spanish Communist Party
PCI	Italian Communist Party
EC	Executive Committee
LP	Labour Party
LSI	Labour and Socialist International, also known as the Second International
TUC	Trades Union Congress
USSR	Union of Soviet Socialist Republics, also known as the Soviet Union

Foreword

INTRODUCTION

Line of March was the first title published by Praxis Press in 1994. This revised edition is being republished to mark the Communist Party's centenary celebrations (1920-2020).

The book is based on an original manuscript written around 1986 by Max Adereth, a communist academic and activist. In 1993, the late Joe Berry passed me a copy of the typescript after an educational dayschool on revolutionary strategy organised by young communists in London.

The noted Marxist economist Ron Bellamy, at the time a member of the leadership of the Communist Party of Britain (CPB), generously provided both a warm personal tribute to Max in the book's preface as well as an exceptionally insightful postscript.

The postscript covered the developments in the tumultuous decade after the main text was written, namely the collapse of the Soviet Union and the socialist states of central and Eastern Europe, as well as the liquidation of the original Communist Party of Great Britain (CPGB) and the re-establishment of the Communist Party of Britain in 1988.

Ron Bellamy's suggestions that in the absence of a common "communist threat" there would be a re-emergence of inter-imperialist rivalries among the Western powers proved to be particularly prophetic.

The initial motivation for publishing the manuscript was to counter the dominant "death of communism" narrative that accompanied the then-almost unchallenged ideas of "the end of history", and a unipolar "New World Order" dominated by the United States.

The second reason was to review the rich but by no means uncomplicated history of British communism; to identify and combat the influences of right-wing revisionism within the British communist movement, while simultaneously resisting a tempting retreat into dogmatism and "revisionism of the left".

1 HISTORICAL AND INTERNATIONAL CONTEXT

In his historical overview, Adereth reminded readers that the Communist Party was not some foreign import, regardless of how much its founders were immediately inspired by the triumph of the October Revolution of 1917 in Russia. The party's roots lay much deeper in the pioneering experience of the British working-class.

The Industrial Revolution of the late 18th and early 19th centuries in Britain gave birth to mass trade unions and workers' self-managed co-operative societies. The early 1800s saw the emergence of early utopian socialist thinkers, such as Robert Owen, and attempts to create socialistic communities such as Owen's own project at New Lanark in Scotland. Most importantly, the 1830s and 1840s witnessed the rise of the Chartists, the world's first mass working-class political force. This coincided with the arrival in Britain first of Frederick Engels and then Karl Marx.

Engels became a regular contributor to the early British socialist press soon after his arrival in Manchester in 1842. He wrote several articles on French and German communism for Robert Owen's *New Moral World* as well as for Chartist leader Feargus O'Connor's mass circulation *Northern Star*. These articles appeared in the aftermath of the huge strike wave of 1842 that involved as many as 500,000 workers across Britain. This was a strike where economic and political demands began to overlap. To use an expression that Marx coined a few years later, a *class in itself* was also becoming *a class for itself*.

Lenin wrote of Engels' early Mancunian years:

> Engels got to know the proletariat in England, in the centre of English industry, Manchester, where he settled in 1842, entering the service of a commercial firm of which his father was a shareholder. Here Engels not only sat in the factory office but wandered about the slums in which the workers were cooped up, and saw their poverty and misery with his own eyes. But he did not confine himself to personal observations. He read all that had been revealed before him about the condition of the British working class and carefully studied all the official documents he could lay his hands on. The fruit of these studies and observations was the book which appeared in 1845: *The Condition of the Working Class in England*.

Marx visited Engels in Britain in 1845 and the two men collaborated on two key texts that year, *The German Ideology* and *The Holy Family*, which marked significant steps in their joint evolution toward scientific socialism. Marx and Engels were inspired by the intellectual and social discussions of British thinkers. They were especially struck by the pro-working class conclusions of some of these philosophers and economists.

Engels later recalled:

> At that time Marx had never yet been in the reading room of the British Museum. Apart from the libraries of Paris and Brussels, besides my books and extracts seen during a six weeks' journey in England we made together in the summer of 1845, he had only examined such books as were obtainable in Manchester. The literature in question was, therefore, by no means as inaccessible in the forties as it may be now.

In *The Holy Family*, they paid their respects to a series of Scottish and English philosophers from Duns Scotus, Bacon, Hobbes, and Locke to Bentham. "Materialism", they wrote, "is the natural-born son of Great Britain."

The Welshman Robert Owen, the text continued:

> proceeded from Bentham's system to found English communism. Exiled to England, the Frenchman Cabet came under the influence of communist ideas there and on his return to France became the most popular, if the most superficial, representative of communism. Like Owen, the more scientific French Communists, Dézamy, Gay and others, developed the teaching of materialism as the teaching of real humanism and the logical basis of communism.

Marx and Engels considered Etienne Cabet one of the great figures of early French communism. For many decades, Britain was a natural destination for revolutionary exiles from the European mainland, including two of Marx's son-in-laws – Paul Lafargue and Charles Longuet.

Although *Manifesto of the Communist Party* appeared first in the German language in 1848, its text was typeset in Drury Lane in London's Covent Garden and then printed a few miles to the east at 46 Liverpool Street in Bishopsgate. The first English translation – by the remarkable Scottish Chartist Helen Macfarlane – appeared in 1850 in George Julian Harney's socialist periodical *Red Republican*. This was the first time a Marxist programme of any kind appeared before British working-class activists.

Marx and Engels spent the following years acquainting themselves with the emerging working-class movement in Britain and the rapid development of the most advanced capitalist economy of its day. Marx drew heavily on the theoretical contributions of two eminent British economists, Adam Smith and David Ricardo. Lenin was later to describe "English [sic] political economy" as one of the three sources of Marxism, along with French socialism and German philosophy.

Thanks to the immense research material available in the British Library Marx was able to craft the detail of his greatest work *Capital*. Paul Lafargue, Marx's son-in-law, wrote that:

> in order to write the 20 pages or so on English factory legislation in *Capital* he [Marx] went through a whole library of Blue Books containing reports of commissions and factory Inspectors in England and Scotland. He read them from cover to cover, as can be seen from the pencil marks in them. He considered those reports as the most important and weighty documents for the study of the capitalist mode of production. He had such a high opinion of those in charge of them that he doubted the possibility of finding in another country in Europe 'men as competent, as free from partisanship and respect of persons as are the English factory inspectors'. He paid them this brilliant tribute in the Preface to *Capital*.

It was in London too that the First International, the International Working Men's Association, was founded in St Martin's Hall in September 1864. Britain also hosted refugees from the Paris Commune as well as two congresses of the Russian Social Democratic Labour Party (RSDLP). These were the historic second congress of 1902, where the party split into Bolshevik and Menshevik factions, and the RSDLP's fifth Congress of 1907.

In the early 20th century, Lenin edited the RSDLP paper *Iskra* in London, sharing the office and printshop of *Justice*, the newspaper of Britain's Social-Democratic Federation (SDF). The SDF later became the British Socialist Party (BSP) and would eventually become a significant actor in the communist unification process of 1920-21. The *Iskra* office today is the Lenin Room, part of the Marx Memorial Library in Clerkenwell Green.

During his times in London, Lenin often visited the London home of Theodore Rothstein, an exile from Tsarist Russia. Rothstein had initially joined the Social Democratic Federation in 1895 but also later joined the RSDLP, where he sided with the party's Bolshevik wing.

Rothstein was a regular writer for the SDF's *Justice* newspaper and theoretical journal *The Social Democrat*, as well as the BSP paper *The Call*. He was named *Pravda*'s first London correspondent in 1912. He opposed the chauvinist line of Henry Hyndman in the SDF, later renamed British Socialist Party, and stood with the BSP's internationalist and anti-war forces throughout the first world war.

Rothstein also entered the early communist unity debates. In some of his writings in late 1919, just before leaving for Russia, he strongly attacked both the:

> Revisionists, on the one hand, for what we used to call 'parliamentary cretinism,' and the Anarchists, on the other, for their rejection of parliamentary warfare... So long; as the masses are still interested in parliament and attach importance to its proceedings, we should be fools, if not criminals, if we abstained from making use of its opportunities.

This prefigures the virtually identical presentation of these arguments by Lenin in his *Left-wing Communism: An Infantile Disorder* published several months later.

These varied influences predate the formation of the Communist Party of Great Britain in July 1920. The CPGB was a party with national roots but an internationalist perspective. In fact, it is no exaggeration to say that the development of Marxism-Leninism cannot be understood without these British influences.

Later influences, through the CPGB's affiliation with the Communist International, are too often presented in monochrome, with a subservient CPGB whipped into line by Moscow. More recent historical research presents a more complicated picture, one more of selective interpretation and implementation of Comintern guidance as well as sometimes ill-advised, but not always reluctant, acceptance.

However, the Comintern actively intervened in combatting 'left-wing communism' in Britain, it insisted that the CPGB do its utmost to champion the rights of the oppressed peoples of the British Empire, that the party devote greater attention to Marxist theory and intensify the political education of its militants. These proved to be invaluable contributions to the wider British labour movement.

On the other side of the balance sheet, Adereth noted that the early periods of the CPGB's history were characterised by an uncritical and adulatory view of the socialist countries, particularly during the Stalin era. This led the party not only to promote the tremendous social gains and economic achievements during the construction of the early socialist states but also to justify many of the crimes committed in the name of defending those genuine gains against enemies both real and imagined.

It also led the party during this time to rather mechanically adopt other state models. Firstly these were variants of "Soviet power", then in the first edition of the *BRS*, a form of "People's Democracy", which was being applied, with varying degrees of success in Eastern Europe and Asia.

In the latter case, CPGB leader Harry Pollitt spent some time in Moscow, discussing various concepts and formulations with Soviet communist party theoreticians, culminating in face-to-face meetings with Stalin, who suggested various reformulations, but who did not fundamentally disagree with the draft Pollitt took with him.

Writing as he was at the beginning of the period of glasnost and perestroika, Adereth expresses admiration for Mikhail Gorbachev's early reforms. However, these proved to be ineffectual in correcting the accumulated deformations of Soviet socialism and ultimately fostered ideological and political trends committed to destroying socialism outright.

The "post-Soviet" period from 1989-91 onward has witnessed the resurgence of neo-liberal anti-communism, outright neo-nazism and vicious anti-semitism in the former socialist states. In addition, the shift in global balance of forces led to a renewed round of aggressive wars launched by Western imperialist powers from the Balkans, to North Africa and the Middle East.

However naïvely expressed at times, the CPGB's post-1956 view, that despite serious deformations, the European socialist countries continued to represent a bulwark of peace, anti-fascism and socio-economic progress, creating a genuine alternative and international counter-weight to Western capitalism, needs to be evaluated in greater detail than is possible here. However, the merits of those arguments cannot be summarily dismissed.

2 CONCEPTUAL QUESTIONS

By adopting *The British Road to Socialism* in the postwar period, did British communists embrace a "parliamentary road to socialism" as some of its leftist critics maintain? Did the Communist Party commit itself to an entirely "peaceful path" rather than the armed road that proved successful elsewhere? These remain fundamental objections to the *BRS* but are based on certain misconceptions and misinterpretations of these terms.

Communists and Parliament

In 1922, the Communist International adopted a Thesis on Workers' Governments. The theses not only urged communist parties to participate in parliamentary elections, as Lenin had earlier urged, but also raised the possibility that in certain circumstances communist parties could become the dominant parliamentary force that could result in "revolutionary workers' governments". This suggested an alternative path to power from the insurrectionary model, where revolutionary forces led risings against established governments, just as the Bolsheviks had done against the Provisional Government in Russia in 1917.

A second variant, a workers' and peasants' government, was advocated for less developed countries, where communists might achieve parliamentary majorities in alliance with parties representing the peasantry.

Both types of revolutionary governments could become centres of struggle for state power as a whole, with revolutionary forces using their consti-

tutional legitimacy and powers, including the arming of working people, to rally support in the face of an inevitable backlash from the existing ruling class. Although full-scale civil war was not seen as inevitable., the ensuing struggle could then result in the victory of the revolutionary forces.

A third option was mooted, "liberal workers" governments. In Australia in 1922, the right-wing reformist Australian Labour Party won the election and formed a government. It was assumed that the same could happen in Britain. In fact, in 1924 a minority Labour government did take office. Such reformist governments could not be expected to launch a major struggle for winning state power, but it could even in these restricted circumstances "erode bourgeois power" and provide a springboard for further advance. Simply put, Communist demands were to support those policies that were in the interest of the working class, denounce those that favoured capitalism and use the opportunity to politically educate the Labour voting masses on the need for a revolutionary break with capitalism.

Communists in Britain therefore offered critical support for Labour candidates and for the return of Labour governments despite their right-wing leadership and policies. This was a perspective that the CPGB only deviated from during the sectarian "Third Period".

In the various editions of the later *British Road to Socialism*, the CPGB argued that the "existing machinery" of the British Parliamentary system could not simply be taken over and used by a working-class electoral majority. The CPGB made clear that its focus was on transforming or *converting* the House of Commons (whose very name illustrates the complicated class origins of this institution of the British state) into an elected assembly genuinely representing the popular will of the mass of the British working class and its allies.

As the very first *BRS* stated and later versions reiterated, the unelected House of Lords would need to be abolished, the power of the monarchy to approve or block legislation would be ended and the monarchy itself would be abolished, while the conservative bureaucracy of the Civil Service would have to be transformed through replacement of key personnel. Furthermore the CPGB insisted on the need to create national parliaments for the peoples of Scotland and Wales as well reinforcing the power and democratic accountability of local and district councils.

All of this, however, would be dependent on sustaining a militant mass movement organized outside parliamentary institutions in workplaces and communities, through the mobilisation of the mass organisations of the working class; trade unions, trades councils, co-ops and so on.

The communist aim was to combine a powerful *extra-parliamentary* force to support the conversion of the main *elected* representative institution – the House of Commons in the British case – from a talking shop into a working body that would be genuinely representative of the mass of the British people.

As Lenin put it in *State and Revolution*:

> Once again, we must say: the lessons of Marx, based on the study of the Commune, have been so completely forgotten that the present-day "Social-Democrat" (i.e., present-day traitor to socialism) really cannot understand any criticism of parliamentarism other than anarchist or reactionary criticism.

> The way out of parliamentarism is not, of course, the abolition of representative institutions and the elective principle, but the conversion of the representative institutions from talking shops into "working" bodies." The Commune was to be a working, not a parliamentary, body, executive and legislative at the same time. (emphasis added).

However, such a "conversion of the representative institutions" would hardly go uncontested by the ruling class and its state bureaucracy. So this leads us naturally to the second issue. Are there ways to overcome the resistance of the ruling class – which will never relinquish power voluntarily – there a way to over "peaceful" path to socialism, or is a civil war between the working class and the ruling class inevitable?

'Peaceful' paths to socialism?

The polarization between the concepts of "armed" and "peaceful" paths to socialism is often unhelpful. All successful armed struggles, such as the popular insurrection of the Cuban Revolution, the victories of the Chinese communists in their Civil War against the Guomindang, and those of the Vietnamese revolutionaries, which combined both elements of civil war and national liberation war, were the culmination of decades of struggles that also took a variety of peaceful forms. These included things such as simple political agitation and propaganda, mass demonstrations, general strikes and even, where circumstances permitted, electoral campaigns.

During a period of armed struggle in Russia, Lenin pointed out:

> Marxism differs from all primitive forms of socialism by not binding the movement to any one particular form of struggle. It recognises the most varied forms of struggle; and it does not "concoct" them, but only generalises, organises, gives conscious expression to those forms of struggle of the revolutionary classes which arise of themselves in the course of the movement. Absolutely hostile to all abstract formulas and to all doctrinaire recipes, Marxism demands an attentive attitude to the mass struggle in progress, which, as the movement de-

velops, as the class-consciousness of the masses grows, as economic and political crises become acute, continually gives rise to new and more varied methods of defence and attack. Marxism, therefore, positively does not reject any form of struggle.

At the 1957 and 1960 World Conference of Communist Parties, a nuanced position was adopted. This recognized, as the first *BRS* had done, the possibility of revolutionary changes being carried forward in certain countries without "civil war". The declaration however suggested a number of conditions that needed to be met for such a development to proceed. It stressed that communists could never on principle renounce the use of armed force to defend the mass movement against counter-revolutionary violence. The critical element was to make a concrete analysis of the level and stages of class struggle at any given moment and to choose the optimum forms of struggle that conformed with them. The declaration stated:

> In the event of the exploiting classes resorting to violence against people, the possibility of non-peaceful transition to socialism should be borne in mind. Leninism teaches, and experience confirms, that the ruling classes never relinquish power voluntarily. In this case, the degree of bitterness and the forms of the class struggle will depend not so much on the proletariat as on the resistance put up by the reactionary circles to the will of the overwhelming majority of the people, on these circles using force at one or another stage of the struggle for socialism.

> The actual possibility of the one or the other way of transition to socialism in each individual country depends on the concrete historical conditions.

Unfortunately, after these Moscow conferences major divisions appeared within the international communist movement. One of the negative results was the tendency to make an absolute principle of one or other forms of struggle. Those revolutionaries who took the Chinese Revolution – and later the Cuban Revolution – as models, tended to absolutise the armed forms of struggle.

However, many insurrectionary groups in Asia and Latin America, which mechanically implemented these models, failed, due in large part to their refusal to objectively assess the specific conditions of struggle in the countries concerned.

The second negative tendency, which eventually gave rise to "Eurocommunism" in a number of mass communist parties in developed capitalist countries, stressed the constitutional and parliamentary paths – even at the expense of certain forms of extra-parliamentary struggles. As Adereth shows, in Britain the revisionist wing of the CPGB continually downgraded the key role of working-class struggles, which they derided as "economism", counterposing them with the struggles of "new social forces".

The latest version of *Britain's Road to Socialism* notes the need to prepare in advance for ruling-class sabotage and resistance and the need for tactical flexibility in developing appropriate forms of mass struggle:

> The ruling class will battle for its very survival and can be expected to use every weapon at its disposal against the revolutionary movement and the left government.

> For example, as in the 1970s, private armies might form under the direction of ex-military chiefs, supported by big business leaders and sections of the mass media. This possibility will be reduced by the measures already proposed to democratise and unionise the armed forces and to break monopoly power, not least in the mass media.

> Direct foreign military intervention against a left government in Britain with mass support is unlikely. Nevertheless, there is the possibility that US and NATO military bases in Britain might become centres of intrigue and subversion. Once again, this underlines the need for an elected left government to move swiftly to close all foreign military bases in Britain and withdraw from NATO and EU armed forces.

> The key factor in this decisive, third stage of the revolutionary process will be the balance of forces outside parliament and in society as a whole. In particular, it will be vital to mobilise the popular anti-monopoly alliance – led by the organised working class – to uphold popular sovereignty and help the elected government to enforce its policies.

> The extent to which this process involves physical or military violence will depend upon the revolutionary movement having the best strategy to minimise the capacity for resistance of the capitalist class. As the working class invariably bears the brunt of counter-revolutionary violence, it is the duty of all serious revolutionaries to devise such a strategy, rather than propose simplistic notions of violent insurrection and armed struggle.

> In any event, there can be no question: the democratically elected left government will use all the official and popular forces at

its disposal to crush each and every attempt at military subversion, rebellion or invasion.

To summarise; the distinction between peaceful and armed paths is useful only in the sense that on each road to socialism and during each stage on that road certain forms of struggle predominate over others. However, since the "peaceful", option as understood by the communist movement historically, allows for such a wide spectrum of scenarios of violence and conflict that fall short of civil war, this sets a rather high bar. It is naturally confusing to the general reader who understands the term peaceful to be the complete absence of violence.

Chilean communist leader Jorge Insunza warned of the dangers of abstractly dividing revolutionary strategy into two separate, even diverging, streams. Drawing on the experience of the overthrow of Salvador Allende's government in 1973, he later wrote: "Our experience confirms that the roads of revolution – peaceful and armed – cannot and should not be regarded as mutually exclusive. Treating them as opposite poles is dangerous to the success of the revolutionary process."

3 DEVELOPMENTS IN 21st CENTURY

A seventh edition of the programme in 2000 was renamed *Britain's Road to Socialism*. An eighth edition was adopted in July 2011 and further amended in 2020. Readers can visit the Communist Party of Britain's website at communist-party.org.uk to for copies of the latest version.

Since there have been a number of significant changes in the international and domestic situation since Ron Bellamy's 1994 postscript. We will mention only a few of the most significant here. The quotes heading each section are from the 2020 draft edition of the *BRS*.

a] Uniting the Left

The combined forces of the extra-parliamentary mass movements, the trade unions and the Labour left … propelled left MP Jeremy Corbyn to victory in 2015 and 2016.

It now remains to be determined whether the socialist and social-democratic trends are strong enough with trade union support to take and maintain full control of the Labour Party. The working class and peoples of Britain need a mass political party, based on the labour movement, that can win general elections, form a government and implement substantial reforms in their interests. {p23}

Throughout the 1990s and into the first decades of the 21ˢᵗ century, the CPB continued to emphasise the need for left unity and the central importance of the Labour Party left. This was at a time when the triumph of Tony Blair's 'New Labour' led some to conclude that the battle to turn the Labour Party leftward was lost forever. The Socialist Labour Party, Respect, the Scottish Socialist Party, Left Unity and other initiatives achieved some fleeting successes but were never able to form coherent mass alternatives to the Labour Party, as communists warned.

The premature dismissal of the Labour Party as a field of struggle was largely abandoned once left Labour MP Jeremy Corbyn was elected and then re-elected Labour leader. The Labour Party quickly became the largest left party in Europe in terms of membership. In some quarters, despair was simply replaced by euphoria, the Labour left seemed unstoppable.

While the CPB and *Morning Star* expressed their strong support for Corbyn's overall project, key differences remained. This was especially true over support for membership of the European Union, a position held by many Corbyn supporters as well as centrists and the right-wing. The disastrous pre-election abandonment of Labour's previous pledge to respect the Leave vote in the 2016 referendum delivered a stunning but predictable defeat inn 2019 and provided a pivot for the right-wing to regain leverage inside the Labour Party.

As this book goes to press, Keir Starmer, Corbyn's successor has begun the push-back against the socialist policies Corbyn advocated. The right-wing of the LP has quickly regrouped and the Labour left has retreated in some disorder. Already the evidence is emerging of the deliberate and conscious sabotage by right-wingers of their own party Corbyn.

It is inevitable that there are again renewed calls to abandon Labour to the right. Some conclude that the Corbyn movement was the left's last chance and that the left must break away to form a new party.

However, the history of the CPGB offers some valuable counter-points. The party's brief period of sectarian isolation took place when its influence in the pits, factories and among the unemployed was many times that of comparable contemporary left-sectarian groups. While some important organizational gains did occur, such as the launch of the *Daily Worker*, the CPGB failed to break through as a party capable of leading mass struggle in this period. Despite the betrayals of the General Strike and the National Government, the overwhelming majority of the working class remained unimpressed by the CPGB's abstract calls for Soviet power.

Today, hundreds of thousands of people have come into political activity during the past few years through the shift to the left in the Labour Party. However, the communist view is that left unity is not merely a question of numbers nor even mass mobilization. Both are necessary but not sufficient. Effective activity needs to be based on identifying common tactical and strategic goals.

As far as the more recent editions of the *BRS* are concerned, greater attention has been placed on identifying these common goals. The concept of a Left-Wing Programme (LWP) was introduced to complement the Alternative Economic and Political Strategy (AEPS), an anti-monopoly platform that had been in development for several decades.

> In seeking to challenge and defeat British state-monopoly capitalism, the AEPS must engage with the class struggle on the economic, political and ideological fronts. It must also propose the kind of policies that can promote the interests of the working class and the mass of the peoples of Britain, making inroads into the wealth and power of the capitalist class. Such a left-wing programme (LWP) would therefore need to embrace important economic, environmental, social, cultural, financial, democratic and foreign policy questions. [p28]

b] Environmental perspectives

> In the first half of the 21st century, after more than 200 years of capitalist domination, humanity faces a series of inter-related crises that imperil the very existence of our species on this planet. Two billion of the Earth's seven billion population lack adequate nutrition, sanitation, healthcare and education. The world faces a catastrophic energy crisis, as finite resources are depleted without the development of safe, sustainable alternatives. At the same time, burning fossil fuels is warming the planet and changing climate patterns with potentially disastrous consequences for us all. Wars continue to devastate human lives on a massive scale, while the existence and proliferation of weapons of mass destruction carry the threat of even greater horrors to come.

> Communists hold capitalism primarily responsible for these crises, for taking the planet and its peoples towards the edge of the abyss. [p4]

Communists in the early part of the 20th century had little idea of the long-term negative effects of industrialisation. Marxists need to ensure economic growth is environmentally sustainable. While future socialist societies will continue to greatly expand the "productive forces" to resolve issues of poverty and backwardness, this has to be done in a planned manner by protecting the planet's eco-system, developing processes that reduce and eliminate waste thereby ensuring the future of generations to come.

c] Effects of Capitalist Restoration in Eastern Europe

The increasing failure to mobilise the party, the working class and the people to solve these and other economic, social and political problems led eventually to stagnation and political collapse in eastern Europe and the Soviet Union, from 1989. There were no significant mass movements to defend the socialist system against counter-revolution.

Yet the weaknesses and failures of the Soviet model of socialism have since been overtaken by the calamities of capitalist restoration. Public economic property has passed into the hands of Western TNCs, state bureaucrats and home-grown gangsters. Millions of workers have lost their jobs, pensions and trade union rights. Public and welfare services have collapsed. The peoples of the former Soviet Union experienced the biggest reductions in life expectancy ever recorded. National and ethnic differences have exploded into terrorism and war. In some countries, the brutal trafficking and sexual exploitation of women became widespread. [p18]

The *BRS* has expanded on some of the insights of the party's 1992 debates, referred to by Ron Bellamy in his texts written in 1994. As long as Boris Yeltsin remained in power, Russia remained on relatively friendly terms with the US, which played the major role in securing Yeltsin's grip on power, faced as he was with a strong challenge from the Communist Party of the Russian Federation.

Subsequent developments, however, have shown that not all of those who supported capitalist restoration were content for Russia to remain as an entirely subordinate satellite of the West. The rise and consolidation of power in the hands of Vladimir Putin, Yeltsin's hand-picked successor, reveals the desire of sections of the new Russian bourgeoisie to reassert domestic sovereignty and increase regional influence, bringing it into repeated conflict with the US and European imperialist powers. This is illustrated in various trade sanctions, political boycotts, the dangerous escalation of conflict in eastern Ukraine, the taking back of Crimea, as well as Putin's independent foreign policy in the Middle East and Asia.

The role of "European integration" – in plain terms the absorption of former socialist countries into the economic framework of the European Union and the military framework of Nato – gathered pace after 1994. Directly and indirectly, this resulted in both the war in Yugoslavia and the crises of the Kiev governments, among other events. There needs to be a great deal of further study and research into the specific processes of capitalist restoration in the USSR and elsewhere.

d] Europe, war and crisis

> Because European Union fundamental treaties and institutions cannot be radically reformed without unanimous agreement between all member states, a left government in Britain would need to be free from all the neoliberal and anti-socialist provisions of the EU Single Market. It must be able to assert the principle of popular sovereignty in order to develop free and equal trade, commercial and political relations with other countries across the globe – including those in Europe – and to act in solidarity with oppressed peoples, promoting such values in the United Nations and other international bodies. [p38]

As this book goes to press, the UK is no longer formally a member of the European Union but is still subject to a whole raft of EU policies. The CPB consistently opposed the EU from a left and internationalist perspective and warned that failure to respect the Leave vote would fatally undermine Labour's electoral chances. Some sections of the left, which had held anti-EU positions for decades, gradually abandoned this opposition on the grounds that the Brexit camp was dominated by right-wing and xenophobic currents.

The CPB's view was that the right would naturally use widespread antipathy toward the EU demagogically but precisely for that reason the fundamental arguments about democracy and control of the economy – summed up in the term "popular sovereignty" – could not be surrendered to the right. Disastrously this was ignored by the Labour leadership, allowing the very same xenophobic and racist right to appropriate these issues and drive through anti-working class and racist immigration policies.

The now dominant wing of the Conservative Party led by Prime Minister Boris Johnson is clearly set on a new right-wing populist agenda that draws inspiration from the US and a number of European countries. This poses direct dangers for the Labour movement. In particular, it represents a radical challenge to the previously successful policies of the Left – challenges that involve much more active state intervention in periods of economic stagnation and crisis.

However, as in the past, these policies will be vulnerable on an objective level to capitalism's deepening contradictions and the growth of inter-imperialist rivalries. On the subjective front, unmet expectations raised by the populist policies themselves can reveal the class interests behind empty slogans. A firm response demands a radical deepening of mass work by the trade unions, the Labour Party, communists and the broader Left. It also needs these movements to champion *popular* sovereignty – particularly challenging the concentration of capitalist ownership and posing the alternative of popular ownership and control at regional, national and British level.

e] China's rise, US decline?

> China's communists have placed great emphasis on economic
> and social development. State power is being used to combine
> economic planning and public ownership with private capital
> and market mechanisms... So far, state-directed policies have
> lifted more than 700 million people – almost half the popula-
> tion – out of extreme poverty since 1981, a feat unequalled in
> history. The aim of the Communist Party of China (CPC) is to
> build a harmonious, moderately prosperous and sustainable
> socialist society in this, its primary stage... Yet, as the CPC itself
> acknowledges, problems in Chinese society of social inequal-
> ity, inadequate welfare provision, corruption and underdevel-
> oped trade unionism need to be further addressed and recti-
> fied. Advances have been made in extending democratic rights
> without the CPC weakening its leading role in political life.
> The importance of renewing democracy inside the party and in
> wider society should not be underestimated. [p18]

The first edition of the *BRS* was published in 1951, in the immediate aftermath of the Chinese revolution. The assumption at the time and for some
decades afterward, was that as the socialist camp was expanding the international balance of forces was increasingly favourable, especially in limiting
the possibility of outside intervention, economic as well as military, against
a socialist government in Britain.

The drastic shift in international politics after the collapse of the Soviet
Union allowed neo-conservative forces in the USA – such as the Project for
a New American Century – to propose that US imperialism should now
take its apparently unassailable superiority to greater heights by stepping
up regime-change wars and interventions against the remaining socialist
states, but also against a whole host of other nations which were regarded as
insufficiently deferential to Washington. The idea of a unipolar world lead
by the USA was embraced to a greater or lesser degree by both Republicans
and Democrats.

However, China's dramatic economic rise, driven by the calculated policy of creating synergy between state-owned enterprises and market mecha-
nisms, has disrupted US hegemony of the global economy.

Intensified conflicts may result in yet another substantial shift in the
global balance of forces. As this book is being published, the Coronavirus
health crisis is being weaponised by the Trump administration to attack
China on all fronts. The precise outcome is still far too early to predict, however it is obvious that China-US tensions are out in the open.

Nonetheless the *BRS* points to the numerous internal challenges facing
the China, ranging from the need to rebalance economic growth, address

widening social inequality and further democratise China's political system. These may become the defining international questions of the next few decades.

Conclusion

Max Adereth's book makes an invaluable contribution to evaluate the past 100 years of British communism. This is not simply an exploration in the history of a particular section of the British left – as useful as that is – but also a reminder that all history is made by people in circumstances not of their own choosing.

Identifying the strengths and weaknesses of how British communists faced the fundamental questions of state power, class alliances, working-class and left unity, as well as assessing the shifts in the development of British imperialism domestically and internationally will remain critical themes of debate for a considerable time to come.

Kenny Coyle

Preface

The programmes of a Communist Party are forged out of working people's struggles so as to become instruments for shaping the future. Max Adereth's history of the programmes developed by British Communists is at the same time the story of workers' defeats and victories, and of the part played by Communists in them.

Much such history is written today by academic spectators. If they were not alive to be actors in the events they analyse, that is not their fault. But to know how to swim, to estimate the forces and direction of turbulent currents, it is necessary – as Lenin reminded us – first to get into the water. Practical experience is the first condition of objective knowledge. Objectivity, they tell us, is threatened by commitment. Not true. The threat is from blind, unthinking and dogmatic commitment. But that is the very opposite of Marxism as a science.

Max Adereth was able to write the present objective, critical history because he combined scientific thought and action in an exemplary Communist way.

So when I say that this book was his last substantial theoretical contribution to Marxism, the reader must remember that Communists of my generation – and Max was only a little younger – had seen many professional intellectuals and students "come to Marxist theory" under the impact of this or that crisis in capitalism, only to abandon it when capitalism, for the time being, promised security and opportunity.

It is not difficult to show why large groups show such tendencies. But individuals have specific experiences also which lead their convictions to develop in one direction rather than another. Even for ourselves, we can

rarely analyse these processes fully, so it would be impertinent of me to attempt it for Max. But it must be more than a mere guess that what Max did, throughout the long interplay of his practical and intellectual life, shaped the still developing Communist of 1988-89.

He died after a short illness in December 1989 at the age of 69. Almost the whole of his adult life (47 years) had been spent in the Communist Party, which he joined during the Second World War. From April 1988, he and I were members of an advisory committee on inner-party education, set up by the Communist Party of Britain, to begin repairing the damage done by a decade of combined neglect and perversion. The task was not simple. For we respected the conditions on which the Communist Party had been re-established in April 1988, namely the rules and the 1977 programme of the CPGB, which could not democratically be changed until a full Congress in the autumn of 1989. Yet some members had doubts about starting education around a programme which had proved vulnerable to abuse. Max typically adhered to principle. We had to stick to the *BRS*, but a *BRS* as intended by the 1977 Congress that adopted it. Otherwise the opponents of re-establishment would say that we were founding a new party and were "splitters". With combined politeness and incisiveness (sometimes in visible tension!) he set about persuading doubters that this was the only possible course.

Max's path first crossed mine in 1975, when I spoke at his branch in Lancaster. Characteristically, he wrote a letter of thanks: "Please don't take this as mere 'bourgeois' politeness – we mean it." I knew what he meant. For we both worked in circles where politeness often masked the stiletto. He enclosed an article on the working class (see Postscript) with the request: "If you have any further comments to make after re-reading it, whether they are scathingly critical or devastatingly hostile, please do not hesitate to let me have them."

Some 14 years later, we joined forces at a Manchester school on Soviet Reforms, of which Max was a strong supporter. How carefully he had prepared, how well structured his material was, how it drew attention to the arguments, and not to the speaker, how searching the questions he had proposed for discussion!

Max had become the person he was through a wide range of experiences. Professionally, he had taught in a number of universities, concerned with French history and culture and in the development of the French working class. His writing of *The French Communist Party: A Critical History* (1984) was a valuable precursor of the present volume. In that *History*, his clear commitment to the object of his enquiry did not lead him to gloss over difficult issues. I was especially impressed by his account of the terrible dilemma faced by thousands of French Communists in their collapsing army of the summer of 1940. (For at the same time I "commanded" a company of 30 "stone throwers" on Salisbury Plain, with one Bren gun and a handful of rifles to cover a sector of 400 yards.) What attitude should French Communists then take to what their party, with many of its leaders in jail, had decided was an imperialist war? Maybe we all know the answers – 50-odd years on, with hindsight and debate! But with complete honesty Max the historian records his inability to trace any copies of *l'Humanité* for the first critical few days.

Of his other two books, one is about Louis Aragon, Communist and Resistance poet and novelist, whose name is a legend in the French working-class movement. The other is about the vexed problem of commitment in literature, dealing with three of the most important figures of the French post-war scene – Aragon himself, Jean-Paul Sartre, the philosopher and essayist, and the poet Peguy. These I have been unable to read because though they are in the catalogue of my university library they are either on loan or "missing" (either of which would suggest their popularity!)

Alongside and bound up with this was his labour-movement experience. While teaching in New Zealand in 1960-65, where its Communist Party adopted an adventurist Maoist stand on war and peace, Max took part in the formation of the Socialist Unity Party, more realistically aligned. Twenty-five years later, in the CPB EC's Report of Work at our own 1989 Congress, is a message of condolence to us from that party. At the time of his death, he was a member of the North West District Committee of the CPB and its Secretariat, was its organiser for party education, and a branch secretary. He was also a member of the national advisory committee for inner-party education.

Nor was that all. When his union, the AUT, finally affiliated to the TUC in the 1970s, he became AUT delegate to Lancaster Trades Council, member of its Executive, its secretary for several years, and delegate to the Lancashire Federation of Trades Councils – work for which he was proud to hold the TUC's scroll, presented by Len Murray.

In brief, Max belonged to a particular generation of Communists who were also professional intellectuals. It was part of their trade to sit in studies and write. But you must ask what was the content and purpose of what they wrote. We know what Max wrote. And if you left it there – at least for most of them – you would still leave out the fact that they did every task that Communists were called on to do.

This gives Max the right to say: This is the national and international experience from which I wrote the history of our Party's programmes. All Communists and militants have a duty to study it critically and – above all – to turn the words into deeds.

Ron Bellamy

Author's Introduction

The Communist Party (hereinafter the CP) is the only political party in Britain to have offered the labour movement a realistic, detailed programme of advance to socialism. Unlike the Labour Party, which prefers to issue general election manifestoes, and unlike the various ultra-left groups, which so far have never gone beyond generalities and slogans, the CP has taken the trouble to outline the steps which, in its opinion, will constitute a British road to socialism.

Whatever the limitations and faults of the various programmes it has put out from time to time (roughly every decade or so), it is a fact that they are the only ones of their kind, and as such they deserve the attention of both socialist militants and political analysts.

What characterises all these programmes is a commitment to revolutionary Marxism-Leninism, ie to the theory and practice of the class struggle in modem conditions. Such a commitment has involved the working out of policies based on the leading role of the working class in the broad popular alliance against capitalism, on the necessary links and bonds of solidarity existing between the working class and revolutionary movements in this country and those in other countries, and on the need to put socialism on the agenda as the only viable alternative to a system which breeds unemployment, poverty, crises, curtailment of democracy and the threat of war.

The first aim of the present study is to bring out the continuity of the Communist approach and of the Communist Party's strategy, whilst at the same time showing the important changes which circumstances and deeper study imposed, and the various mistakes, some serious, some less so, which British Communists made in the elaboration of their strategy.

In the last few years, especially since the early Eighties, a revisionist[1] group inside the Communist Party of Great Britain, labelled "Eurocommunist" by friend and foe alike, managed to gain increasing control of the party machine and to shift the party away from what had until then constituted its distinctive revolutionary identity. At the 39th Congress, held in May 1985, the Euro-communists succeeded in becoming the strongest force, numerically and ideologically, on the party's Executive Committee.

Under their influence, the CPGB became, not only different from what it was in the past, but actually opposed (sometimes openly, sometimes more surreptitiously) to the basic values in which it had believed since its foundation.

The second aim of this study is to show the contrast between Euro-communism and all the CPGB programmes put forward so far, including the 1978 version of The British Road to Socialism. Despite the fact that a number of Eurocommunists took part in the drafting and writing of this version, an unbiased reading of its text shows that it is, like its predecessors, the revolutionary programme of a revolutionary party, and this is due in no small measure both to the rank-and-file members in 1977-78 and to the fact that at the time a majority of EC members had not yet accepted Euro–communism without any reservations.

The present book is divided into two parts, historical and analytical.

The first one is not intended as a potted history of the CPGB[2] but as the necessary background against which the party's successive programmes must be assessed. A very brief summary of each of these programmes is included in this first section.[3] The second part analyses the evolution of the CPGB's strategy with regard to the key issues facing the movement. Without overlooking weaknesses and inadequacies, this section tries to show that at each stage of its history, the CPGB, guided by Marxism Leninism, was able to put forward a strong case for Socialism in Britain.

The following pages deal with issues which are highly controversial. I have tried to present them as objectively as possible, but the reader has already guessed that I write as someone who is, and has been, involved in the debates which I am reporting, the post-war ones at any rate.

Far from taking the view that objectivity depends on scholarly detachment, I believe that this involvement has helped me to get a better appreciation of the issues at stake. Underlying Marx's famous statement that "philosophers have only interpreted the world in various ways, the point, however, is to change it," is the understanding that involvement in the struggle for change is a necessary condition for understanding the struggle itself.

NOTES

[1] Revisionism is the name given to all theories which claim to "revise" Marxism but in fact reject its revolutionary essence.

[2] See Bibliography at the end for the main histories of the CPGB which have appeared to date.

[3] The aim of these summaries is to provide a brief overall view of each programme. Unfortunately, this has entailed a certain amount of repetition in the second part, but such repetition has been kept to a minimum.

This page intentionally left blank

PART 1

Historical

1 Ancestry

The first step towards the formation of a party of the British working class was taken between 1836 and 1840 when the London Working Men's Association, founded in 1836, adopted a Petition or Charter (1837) and eventually became the National Charter Association (1840).

The Charter demanded male universal suffrage, annual Parliaments, vote by secret ballot, payment of MPs, equal electoral districts, and abolition of property qualifications for MPs. Chartism declined after 1848, having failed to achieve its six points at the time, but its importance lies in the fact that it was "the first independent political struggle waged by the working class anywhere in the world".[1]

The next step was the formation of the Labour Party, founded by trade unionists who wanted to send members of their own class to Parliament and by socialist groups which had been set up in the 19th century independently of the unions.

The Labour Party was thus the first attempt to bring together the industrial wing and the political wing of the movement. The former was represented by the Trade Union Congress (TUC), set up in 1868, and by a number of co-operative societies such as that of the Rochdale Pioneers. The latter was represented by three bodies – the Social Democratic Federation (SDF), founded in 1884 by Henry Hyndman; the Fabian Society, founded also in 1884 by GB Shaw, HG Wells and Sydney and Beatrice Webb; and the Independent Labour Party (ILP), founded in 1893 by Tom Mann, John Burns and Keir Hardie. The SDF claimed to be Marxist, but it had a narrow interpretation of Marx's doctrine; the Fabians concentrated on social research and believed in "gradualism"; the ILP's ideology was a form of Christian humanitarianism and pacifism.

In 1900, following a TUC call, all these industrial and political groups met under the name of the Labour Representation Committee (LRC) with the aim of ensuring the return to the House of Commons of working-class MPs. In 1906 the LRC became a proper political party, the Labour Party (LP), but it kept its federal character and, initially, membership of the party was only through one of its constituent bodies.

The Labour Party had no official doctrine, but its outlook and practice were wholly reformist, in the sense that it fought for partial reforms under capitalism rather than for the abolition of the system. This was bound to antagonise those of its members who belonged to the more militant and radical socialist groups. For example, in 1911 the SDF became the British Socialist Party (BSP) and immediately decided to leave the Labour Party. However, in 1916, it reapplied for membership and was readmitted. Another group which was hostile to the LP's reformism was the Socialist Labour Party (SLP), founded in 1903 by people who had been expelled from the SDF; many of its members left it in 1920 to set up the Communist Unity Group (CUG). On the eve of the First World War and during the war itself, there was a proliferation of small revolutionary groups in Britain. In 1920, most of them amalgamated and founded the Communist Party of Great Britain (CPGB).

2 Foundation of the CPGB (1920-21)

The four factors which led to the foundation of the CPGB were the growth of militancy in the British labour movement from 1900 to 1920, the First World War, the 1917 Russian Revolution and the foundation of the Communist International (Comintern or CI) in 1919.

Details of working-class militancy at the beginning of this century can be found in almost any book dealing with that period.[2] What was striking was that the workers' struggles, often spontaneous, received little or no support from the reformist Labour and TUC leaders.

The movement was badly in need of a party capable of linking together all the disconnected struggles that were taking place in order to launch a united, planned offensive against capitalism, but no such party existed. The Labour Party continued to be an electoral machine, while the many socialist groups, Marxist or otherwise, continued to be fragmented and largely isolated from the people.

The clash between the reformist leaders and the militant rank and file was aggravated by the First World War as it became a conflict between those who supported the war effort and those who opposed it. In theory, all the parties of the Labour and Socialist International (LSI) should have been against the war since they had solemnly pledged, at various international congresses, to fight against their own capitalist governments in war time, but in practice all of them, with the exception of the Russian Bolsheviks, supported their respective rulers in the belief that "national defence" was a "sacred duty."

In Britain, the Labour leaders were no exception, but they soon had to contend with a powerful anti-war movement, both among socialist groups such as the BSP and the ILP and among shop stewards such as those who were active among the Clyde engineers. In 1917, there were also mutinies among the troops.

The October 1917 Russian Revolution added fuel to the already existing revolutionary fire in Britain because it was hailed by many workers as the first victory of their class. This is how Harry Pollitt described the effect it had upon him:

> When the news of the Russian Revolution on November 7 1917, came through... I was working in a little shop in Swinton, Lancashire. I had read a little of Marx, but never anything of Lenin. I had never heard of Stalin, but I feel now what I felt then. "The workers have done it at last."... the thing that mattered to me was that lads like me had whacked the bosses and the landlords, had taken their factories, their lands and their banks... All I knew was that the workers had conquered, were the top dogs somewhere in the world. That was enough for me. These were the lads and lasses that I must support through thick and thin.[3]

Soon after the October Revolution, seen by the Bolsheviks as the prelude to the world revolution, Lenin and his followers founded the Third or Communist International, arguing that the Second International had failed the workers in the hour of their greatest need. The Foundation Congress was held in March 1919, and the Second Congress in July 1920. Britain was represented by different organisations, as the CPGB was then in the process of being formed.

The negotiations for the formation of the CPGB were long and protracted. As they have been fully described elsewhere,[4] all that we need to note is that the new party was the result of an amalgamation of heterogeneous groups, each one bringing its own traditions and pet theories into the organisation which was eventually set up.

At the Unity Convention which was held in London in July-August 1920 (in effect, the CPGB's foundation congress), 56% of the delegates came from the BSP, 22% from a new group known as the Communist Unity Group (CUG) and 22% from other bodies.

What the BSP contributed was mainly its genuine commitment to Marxism, even though its Marxism was often bookish and one-sided. The CUG was an offshoot of the SLP, and although it has been set up precisely to combat its parent body's sectarianism and work for the unity of the revolutionary movement, it had by no means been able to shed dogmatic narrow-mindedness, especially because it was violently hostile to the idea of affiliating to the Labour Party.

Of the remaining other bodies, the most important was the South Wales Communist Council (SWCC), a body of militant miners who brought into the movement their experience and their dedication as well as their deep-rooted instinctive suspicion of anything connected with the Establishment, such as Parliament.

The foundation of the CPGB was completed at the Leeds Unity Convention, held in January 1921. Of the additional bodies which took part, the most important were the former Workers' Socialist Federation (WSF), led by the militant suffragette Sylvia Pankhurst, now renamed Communist Party, British Section of the Third International (CP, BSTI) since 1919, and the Communist Labour Party (CLP), of which William Gallacher, a Clyde shop steward, was a member. Both groups brought with them the kind of ultra-leftism which Lenin characterised as "an infantile disorder".[5]

3 Early years (1921-35)

A full account of the CPGB's history up to 1941 can be found in the detailed studies of James Klugmann and Noreen Branson.[6] Here we can only mention the salient points.

The first 14 years of the party's life may be regarded as its period of apprenticeship in becoming a Leninist party of the "new type". According to Lenin and the Comintern, the novelty had to be expressed ideologically, politically, socially, organisationally and morally. Ideologically, what was demanded was uncompromising acceptance and application of Marxism. In this respect, the young CPGB was weak, not because it showed the same disregard for theory as most sections of the British labour movement, but because, initially, its understanding of Marxism was rather superficial and its knowledge of scientific socialism very limited. However, with Comintern guidance, it took steps to put its house in order, so that in June 1925 there were about 90 Marxist Study Centres (involving over 800 members) and by 1934 most party members had received some kind of regular theoretical training.

Politically, a British Leninist party was expected to combine commitment to revolutionary aims and strategy with the ability to work with the reformist Labour Party and inside the reformist-dominated TUC. A similar problem faced most CPs in Europe, but in Britain the original feature of the issue was that it involved a struggle for the CPGB's affiliation to the Labour Party. In spite of the latter's federal nature and constitution, its leaders rejected, with regular monotony, all the applications made by the Communist Party.[7] Another aspect of the Labour-Communist relationship concerned parliamentary elections.

Until 1927, the CPGB put up its own candidates in a small number of constituencies and campaigned for the return of a Labour government, but in 1928 the Comintern launched the "Class Against Class" policy, of which one key element was to regard social-democratic parties[8] and reformist trade unions as part of "the capitalist state apparatus". The result was that in 1929 the CPGB stood 25 candidates and advised voters to demand a "Revolutionary Workers Government". This demand was part of a long document entitled *Class Against Class, The General Election programme of the Communist Party of Great Britain*. Actually, despite its title, this was much more than a general election manifesto since it included a comprehensive list of measures which a revolutionary government would implement. As such a government would be led by Communists, and as by no stretch of the imagination could the 25 Communist candidates be expected to form a government, even if they were all returned, it is obvious that the programme was a long-term one, the first party programme in fact, if not in name.

Another area of the political struggle in which the CPGB was called upon to display a Leninist attitude was anti-imperialism and internationalism. The struggle against British imperialism demanded great courage, not only because the risks of arrest and imprisonment were great, but also because it meant swimming against the tide in a country where pride in the Empire had been instilled among all sections of the people. From the start, the CPGB asserted the colonies' right to independence and it supported national-liberation movements in countless ways.[9]

As for "proletarian internationalism" it involved solidarity with other Communist parties, and above all, with the Soviet Union. The first land of socialism, as it was fondly called, had to be defended against all capitalist attacks in order to show that socialism worked and, from a more practical point of view, in order to ensure the survival and growth of the one country which was "the base of the world revolution".

It cannot be denied that, in common with all other CPs, the CPGB overstressed the USSR's achievements and was blind to its faults. However, it was one of the few sections of the Comintern which warned (guardedly) against the excessive adulation of Stalin and which occasionally protested against some Stalinist excesses.[10]

In the social sphere, a "party of the new type" was expected to have working-class roots and to be able to influence the most advanced sections of the labour movement.

The CPGB's industrial strength was its main redeeming feature from the beginning and it made up for its electoral weakness. In 1923-24, Communists launched the so-called "Minority Movement" in the unions. The movement's secretary Harry Pollitt described it as the "Left Minority *inside* the trade unions", (my emphasis. MA), and whatever sectarian mistakes the movement made, it wisely resisted the temptation of setting up breakaway unions.

During the 1926 General Strike, Communists played an active part on the Councils of Action, and over 1,200 of them were arrested. As the strike gathered momentum, it was called off by the TUC leaders, who thus unwittingly demonstrated the need for a militant revolutionary party in Britain. In the Thirties, at a time of mass unemployment and "depressed areas", the CPGB played a key role in the National Unemployed Workers Movement (NUWM) and in the organisation of Hunger Marches. Both were generally linked to the main trade unions and trades councils.[11]

An important contribution to the spreading of Communist influence among the working people was the launching of the *Daily Worker* in 1930. This was a newspaper with a difference, first, because it relied on ordinary people (worker correspondents) for its news, and secondly, because it saw its role as that of a "political agitator", which provided information as well as education and issued calls to action.[12]

In the organisational field, the CPGB started with a major initial weakness: its branches still had a territorial basis and saw their function mainly as propaganda. In 1925, the CI decided that all CPs should be "bolshevised," ie reorganised on Leninist lines. For the CPGB, the most important aspect of "bolshevisation" was the priority given to factory cells.[13] These were seen as centres of political education and agitation, waging the class struggle around the concrete issues which arose in the workplace, and showing the link between the fight for immediate demands and the wider fight against capitalism.

The final characteristic of a "party of the new type" was the moral quality of its members, in other words, their willingness to be of use to the movement rather than make use of it, their honesty in dealing with members of their class, and their rejection of any form of careerism.

In this respect, the CPGB compared most favourably with any other British political party. Such was the dedication of its members that anti-Communists would refer to them as "fanatics." But these "fanatics" had a wonderful sense of humour, which stood them in good stead when they were hounded and vilified on all sides, as well as a great sense of comradeship. That sense of comradeship occasionally came in for criticism on the part of some Comintern leaders.[14]

In its first programme, the CPGB described itself as a party which embraced the best elements of the working class, "those whose revolutionary spirit and devotion to the cause of their class have made them a vanguard for the working class in its struggle". In 1935, that was no idle boast.

The year 1935 is an important one in the CPGB's history. It marks the end of its apprenticeship period for two reasons, first, because it was in February 1935 that the first party programme was produced and adopted, and secondly, because it was in the summer of 1935 that British Communists began to apply the new strategic line launched by the Comintern, the Popular Front. The first party programme was called *For Soviet Britain*, a title which indicates that, on the one hand, the experience of the Soviet Union was then regarded as a universal model, but that, on the other hand, it was considered important to apply it to original British conditions. *For Soviet Britain* (hereinafter abbreviated to *FSB*) is thus the first attempt by the CPGB to work out a British road to socialism, even if in many respects, such a road was seen as being substantially the same as that taken by the Russian Bolsheviks.

FSB is divided into five parts. The first one, "The Class Struggle in Britain Today," denounces the evils of capitalism and asserts that such a system cannot be ended by the mere winning of a parliamentary majority but by a "workers' revolution". The latter is described as "a continuous process", whose climax is the use of force to unseat the ruling class. Civil war, although considered inevitable because "the capitalists are certain to resist with all their might", is said to be "forced upon the working class".

The second part, "Workers' Dictatorship Is Democracy for the Workers", rejects Parliament on the ground that it is not the real organ of power, and advocates instead Workers' Councils or Soviets. *FSB* is not prescriptive on this point because its authors confidently believe that British workers will spontaneously create their own soviets as they take power into their own hands. Soviet democracy is participatory democracy and in this sense superior to parliamentary democracy. In the socio-economic field, "the workers' dictatorship will make an end of production for profit and will carry on production for use".

The third part, "What the British Soviets Will Do," outlines in some detail the various aspects of the new regime's policies and lays great stress on nationalisation without compensation of the big banks, the big factories, the mines, the transport concerns, and other key sectors of the economy.

The fourth part, "Towards World Socialism", declares that a Soviet Britain will pursue a peaceful foreign policy, grant all British colonies "the right to complete self-determination", put forward proposals for universal peace and disarmament, trade with all nations, especially the USSR, and finally, will, by its very existence, stimulate the revolution in other countries.

The fifth and last part, "The Communist Party," asserts that the CP is essential to lead the revolution because such a party arises from and develops with the class struggle, is based in the scientific teachings of Marx, Engels, Lenin and Stalin, and will never "betray the interests of the working class – for it has no other interests".

4 The Popular Front (1935-39)

At its seventh congress, held in July-August 1935, the Comintern launched the Popular Front strategy as the left's response to the world economic crisis and the rise of fascism. In the late Twenties and early Thirties, the international Communist movement had underestimated the danger of fascism and had concentrated its attacks on social-democracy, which was described as "the moderate wing of fascism".[15] However, after the 1933 victory of fascism in Germany, when Hitler came to power, the Comintern drew the conclusion that fascism would never have won if the working class had been united. It continued to regard – rightly – social-democracy as being mainly responsible for the split, but at the same time, without explicitly saying so, it laid part of the blame on its own sectarianism.[16]

In order to defeat fascism and prevent its victory in the countries which were still ruled by bourgeois democracy, the Comintern advocated a common programme of defensive and offensive actions between Socialists and Communists – the United Front of the working class – as well as a minimum programme of social and democratic reforms to be implemented by a united working class and the middle strata – the Popular Front.

The Popular Front did not mean that Communists had given up their fundamental socialist aim, but rather that they realised that the preservation and extension of existing democratic rights was the best way, the only way at the time, of paving the way for socialism. By putting itself at the head of the anti-fascist front, the working class would demonstrate its ability to lead the whole nation in times of crisis and would therefore be in a better position to win allies when the conditions for socialist revolution have matured.

In France, where the Popular Front strategy originated and was first tested, alliance with the middle strata was at least as important as working-class unity. In Britain, however, the situation was different because, as Harry Pollitt explained:

> Here the decisive majority of the population are industrial workers, the most class conscious are already organised industrially and politically. Our first job is to bring unity within our Labour Movement.[17]

The unity of the labour movement required joint action on a number of urgent issues and made the CPGB's affiliation to the Labour Party more topical than ever. However, both were rejected by the reformist LP and TUC leaders. The CPGB's attempt to build a Popular Front was slightly more successful when appeals were made to the ILP and the Socialist League, both of which agreed to join Communists in issuing a "Unity Manifesto" in January 1937. Its main emphasis was on the need "to revitalise the activity and transform the policy of the Labour Movement".

The most important of the CPGB's activities during the Popular Front period were its successful struggle against British fascism, represented by Mosley's Blackshirts, its campaigns against the Tory-dominated "National" government, its active support of Republican Spain, and its denunciation of the 1938 Munich agreement.[18] Among the most spectacular battles which were waged against British fascists, one must mention the September 1934 counter-demonstration in Hyde Park, the successful heckling of Mosley when he tried to address a meeting at Belle Vue, Manchester, in October, and finally the almost legendary battle of Cable Street in October 1936 when the Mosleyite marchers were completely routed.

The campaigns against the "National" government were directed against its anti-working class policies at home and its appeasement of the fascist dictators abroad.

With regard to Spain, in addition to denouncing non-intervention as a farce, the CPGB was the driving force in forming the British Battalion of the International Brigades, which numbered 2,000 volunteers, half of whom were Communists, and it helped to organise medical and other relief for Spain.

As for the 1938 Munich pact, the only voice denouncing it in Parliament was that of the lone Communist MP William Gallacher, who forcefully protested "against the dismemberment of Czechoslovakia". The CPGB circulated 1 million copies of an appeal written by Pollitt in which Munich was described as a "shameful surrender".

In August 1939, the CPGB issued the draft of a more comprehensive programme than *FSB*. No title was given to it, so we shall simply call it the 1939 *Draft Programme*, abbreviated to *DP*. This draft was to have been discussed at the party's 16th congress, scheduled for October 1939. However, because of the war, the 16th congress was not held until July 1943 and the *DP* was no longer on the agenda.

Although it never got the chance to be debated, it represents a strategic landmark in the CPGB's evolution. Apart from being much more detailed than its predecessor, the 1939 *DP* differs from *FSB* in some important respects.

First, it includes a programme for the immediate present, which takes into account the need to fight fascism and the experience of the Popular Front. In particular, the climax of the people's struggles is seen as the formation of a Labour government "which will hold back the advance of fascism at home and abroad". Although the phrase "Labour government of a new type" is not used, one can say that the concept that it covers is put forward here for the first time.

Secondly, the issue of affiliation to the Labour Party, which was not mentioned by *FSB*, is tackled, not as a temporary tactical measure, but as a key factor in the road to working-class power in Britain.

Thirdly, the 1939 *DP* is still committed to violent revolution, but it is much clearer than *FSB* when it asserts that it is the capitalist class which will be responsible for civil war if it ever takes place. (Cautiously, and by implication only, the 1939 *DP* suggests that we cannot know in advance what form the British revolution will take.)

Finally, although it still advocates soviets rather than Parliament, the 1939 *DP* prefers to speak of workers' councils, and above all, it envisages a positive role for Parliament if a Labour government is elected.

5 The War (1939-45)

During the Second World War the CPGB's stand went through three phases – description of the war as just (September 1939), description of the war as imperialist on both sides (October 1939-June 1941), and description of the war as a people's war against fascism (June 1941-September 1945). During the first phase, the party defended the German-Soviet pact of non-aggression which had been signed in August 1939, but under the leadership of Pollitt, it went on to argue that for the British people, the war against Hitler Nazism was a just one, even though it had been declared by Chamberlain's reactionary government. The party's policy was summed up in the formula "Fight on two fronts", ie both against Hitler abroad and against Chamberlain at home.

In October 1939, when it was learned that the Comintern regarded the war as imperialist on both sides, the CPGB altered its line, replaced Pollitt with Palme Dutt as general secretary, and called for peace. Significantly, however, neither the CI nor the CPGB advocated revolutionary defeatism as in the First World War. There was a noticeable change of emphasis after the fall of France in June 1940 and during the Battle of Britain in the autumn of the same year. The CPGB assured the French people of its solidarity in the fight against the foreign troops occupying their country, whilst at home Communists were active in the campaigns for adequate air-raid protection. The formula which summed up the party's policy was "A people's government for a people's peace". It was around this demand that the People's Convention was held in January 1941. The Convention was attended by 2,000 delegates, representing 1.25 million people. Commenting on the party's peace policy at the time, Dutt wrote in the summer of 1941 (ie after the war had extended to the USSR and changed its character) that the aim was:

> ...in the event of these [peace] proposals being refused, to carry forward the struggle, no longer for imperialist aims but for the aims of the liberation of the peoples.[19]

There is no need to doubt Dutt's sincerity when he asserts that a people's government would have been prepared to continue the war if its peace proposals had been rejected, but it is a pity that such a point was not spelt out at the time. Had that happened, it would have been difficult for the party's enemies, on the left and on the right, to claim that Communists had become appeasers. Controversy is still raging today around the issue of the CPGB's policy before June 1941.[20]

Hitler's attack on the Soviet Union on the 22nd of June 1941 transformed the character of the war, especially after Britain and the USA pledged their support to the USSR. This called for a radical change in CPGB policy. Pollitt, who resumed his post as general secretary, spelt out the significance of the new situation when he declared that "this is a People's War. One that only the common people can and will win."[21] The two slogans which best sum up the party's policies were "Maximum war effort against Hitler Germany" and "Immediate opening of the Second Front in Western Europe". Both involved "national unity," a phrase the party was not afraid to use, arguing that in an anti-fascist war, the interests of all classes in Britain temporarily coincided.

At the same time, the CPGB was under no illusion about the British ruling class and realised only too well that it was their ingrained hatred of communism which was responsible for the delay in opening the Second Front. More importantly, the CPGB always stressed that the driving force in the national alliance was the working class, which alone was anti-fascist without any reservations and ulterior motives.

The CPGB also paid great attention to the post-war situation that would be created after the defeat of fascism. It entertained the mistaken belief that national unity could continue in peace time, but under a Labour majority. It overestimated the significance of the war-time Yalta and Tehran conferences at which the "Big Three" (USA, GB and USSR) promised to co-operate after the war for the establishment of democracy in all countries. However, the CPGB never went as far as Earl Browder who, for a short while, managed to win over the US Communist Party to the view that after Tehran, class divisions had lost their former significance. In fact, when the PCF leader Jacques Duclos criticised Browder, his article was immediately reproduced in *Labour Monthly*, associated with the CPGB. The worst that can be said about the CPGB's erroneous views is that they represented, not a departure from Marxism, but an incorrect application of it. They were based on the belief that the USSR and the popular forces in the west had become strong enough to keep the reactionaries in check and compel them to agree to far-reaching changes.

What was much more positive than British Communists' short-lived semi-Browderite illusions was the new realisation that, as a result of the war in which the common people had played a major part and in which the Soviet Union had established itself as a world power, it was now possible seriously to envisage a peaceful road to socialism in Britain. Such a view, first put forward by Pollitt in his 1945 *Answers To Questions*, was maintained even after the start of the Cold War, and in Pollitt's 1947 *Looking Ahead*, one chapter already bore the significant title of "The British Road to Socialism."

6 The Cold War (1947-56)

The war-time partnership between the western powers and the USSR came to an end in 1947, when President Truman proclaimed that the USA's mission was to lead "the free world" against Communist "totalitarianism". The Communist movement replied with the statement put forward by Zhdanov that the world was now divided into two hostile camps – the camp of war and reaction, headed by the USA, and the camp of peace and socialism, headed by the USSR. Predictably, the Cold War ushered in a period of dogmatic intransigence on both sides, but in spite of this, the Communists of all countries continued to explore the possibility of moving over to socialism by different paths from that followed by the Russian Bolsheviks in 1917. In Eastern Europe, a number of countries which owed their liberation from Nazism to both the struggles of their own peoples and to the advance of Soviet troops embarked upon the road of "People's Democracy".

The main features of this unprecedented development were that working-class rule did not do away with the outward forms of parliamentary democracy and that the government rested on a coalition of Communists and other democratic parties. For western CPs, including the CPGB, this represented an encouragement to work out original national roads to socialism. In 1946, Stalin met a British Labour Party delegation and, according to a report published by Morgan Phillips in the *Daily Herald*, he told them that there were two roads to socialism – the Russian road, which was shorter but bloody, and the British "parliamentary road", which was longer but more peaceful. He added that the followers of Marx and Lenin did not recognise one single road.

It was therefore with Stalin's blessing that in 1951 the CPGB produced the first version of *The British Road to Socialism* (hereinafter abbreviated to *BRS*). This version, drafted by the EC, was slightly amended by the 22nd congress in April 1952. The differences between the texts are minimal, and for all intents and purposes, they can be examined together under the heading of the 1951-52 *BRS*.

The chief novelties were that world war is not the necessary prelude to the socialist revolution, that Britain will follow her own original road to socialism, and that Parliament need not be abolished but transformed to serve the people's interests. The first proposition was not strictly new in as much as Communists had never explicitly asserted that revolutions can only take place in times of war. However, it was a well-known fact that both the Russian revolution and the revolutions which led to "People's Democracy" had occurred in the midst of, or as a result of, a world war. The *BRS* refused to regard this historical fact as a law. Moreover, the unambiguous statement that "a third world war is neither necessary nor inevitable" was an undoubted novelty in the sense that it went beyond the classic Marxist formulation that capitalism breeds war. Not that the warlike tendencies of contemporary capitalism were denied (quite the reverse, in fact), but the *BRS* stressed that the people's united action "can be decisive for the preservation of peace."

The second original feature of the 1951-52 *BRS* is the great stress it lays on the fact that "Britain will reach socialism by her own road" and that the British people "can transform capitalist democracy into a real People's Democracy, transforming Parliament, the product of Britain's historic struggle for democracy, into the democratic instrument of the will of the vast majority of the people". The idea that the British road will be a peaceful one is not spelt out in so many words, but it is implied throughout, especially when the *BRS* asserts that:

> The path forward for the British people will be to establish a People's Government on the basis of a Parliament truly representative of the people.

In order to distinguish the new CPGB approach from the "parliamentary road" as understood by the Labour Party, the 1951-52 *BRS* makes two important points. One is that:

> A people's Parliament and Government which draws its strength from a united movement of the people, with the working class as its core, will be able to mobilise the overwhelming majority of the people for decisive measures to break the economic and political power of the big exploiters.

Secondly, the *BRS* warns that the capitalists will not voluntarily give up their power and privileges, but on the contrary, that they are sure to resist "by all means in their power, including force". And it adds that the people and the government "should be ready decisively to rebuff such attempts".

The 1951-52 *BRS* is a comparatively short document of about 20 pages, divided into seven sections.

The first one, an "Introduction" declares that the people's hopes when they elected a Labour government in 1945 were not fulfilled because Labour in power did not attempt to end capitalism.

The second section, "Peace and friendship with all peoples", outlines the aims of a peaceful socialist foreign policy and includes the statement that a third world war is not inevitable.

The third section, "National Independence of the British people and of all the peoples of the British Empire", denounces Britain's enslavement by US imperialism and demands independence for all the peoples of the British Empire.

The fourth section, "People's Democracy – the path to socialism", is the one which really breaks new ground in putting forward the CPGB's new approach to revolution and to the role of Parliament.

The fifth section, "Socialist Nationalisation" makes out a case for public ownership and contrasts capitalist nationalisation, which is limited to a small sector, does not involve the workers, and pays former owners huge compensation, with socialist nationalisation, which extends to the key sectors of the economy, is fully democratic and relies on workers' management, and allows small compensation for those who co-operate with the people's government, and none for those who resist it.

The sixth section, "Social and Cultural Advance," shows the advantages of socialism in the social and cultural fields.

The seventh and last section, "The Communist Party and the way forward," asserts that the people are the agents of change, but that they need to be led by the party of the working class, based on Marxism.

7 De-Stalinisation and its sequels (1956-58)

What is known as "de-Stalinisation" in the Communist movement began with the 20th Congress of the CPSU in February 1956. At a closed session, Khrushchev delivered his famous "secret speech" denouncing Stalin's arbitrariness and violent repression of all opponents. Not content with debunking a former idol and rejecting any "cult of the individual", the 20th congress encouraged the Communists of all countries to develop their strategy along new lines, paying special attention to the ideas of peaceful coexistence, diversity of national roads to socialism and Socialist-Communist co-operation.

Before the movement could calmly discuss these issues, it was faced with one of the worst crises in its history: the Hungarian events of October. November 1956. As the Hungarian leaders were somewhat reluctant to discard Stalinist practices, the country was seething with discontent and this gave the enemies of socialism their chance to try and overthrow the regime. The Hungarian people and the Communist Party were not strong enough to put down the counter-revolution without Soviet assistance, and on 4 November Soviet troops and tanks entered Budapest and enabled Janos Kadar to form a new government which pledged close alliance with the USSR and radical reforms. Although the leaderships of all CPs defended the Soviet action (after heated debates behind closed doors in some cases, including Britain), a substantial number of rank-and-filers were so appalled that they tore up their party cards.

The CPGB's reaction to all these developments included an inner-party debate and the decision to revise the BRS in the light of recent events. The inner-party debate was sharp, but as it took place before the Hungarian crisis, it did not lead to a split. After Hungary, however, some 7,000 party members (about a fifth of the total membership) resigned, whilst a few others took up such a hostile stand that they were expelled. The situation was so tense that a special congress had to be convened in order to discuss the draft of the revised BRS as well as the thorny issue of inner-party democracy.

The 25th (Special) congress was held in April 1957. The discussion around the revised BRS did not reveal any basic divergences. Nearly all the delegates were happy with the greater emphasis on the possibility of a peaceful path to socialism in Britain and on original British conditions. The section on socialism commanded wide support because it was written "in a warmer and less abstract way".[22] The only controversial section was the one which dealt with future relations between a socialist Britain and the peoples of the Empire. The EC had discussed the matter and agreed by 29 votes to 5 and 1 abstention to propose "voluntary participation in a close fraternal association".[23] Palme Dutt, on behalf of the minority, argued for the deletion of "association" as it might be misunderstood as the Empire under a new label, and he advocated instead "close voluntary fraternal relations".[24] Emile Burns replied that the misunderstanding feared by Dutt was unlikely to occur because "each country would decide for itself whether to come in or not".[25] In the end, the EC majority was defeated, something almost unprecedented in the CP, and it was Dutt's formulation which was adopted. Apart from the importance of the issue itself, it was a novel sight to have EC members arguing among themselves at a public congress.

By far the most controversial issue was that of inner-party democracy. Although everyone agreed about its importance as part of the de-Stalinisation process, there were sharp disagreements about its operation. As the commission appointed to deal with this issue was not unanimous, the delegates had before them two reports, one signed by a minority of three, and the other by a majority of 12, of whom three had reservations, which they stated. The minority report demanded that "minorities on higher committees shall be free to fight for their point of view within the Party".[26] The majority report, on the other hand, argued that this amounted to the legalising of factions. The majority report was endorsed by congress.

After the 25th congress, discussion went on throughout the CPGB about the revised draft of the *BRS*, and the programme finally came out at the beginning of 1958. It begins with an Introduction which states that socialism alone "can solve the problems of the British people" and that this new society will be built by the people "led by the working class". The Introduction is followed by five chapters. The first one, "Our Aim Is Socialism," repeats the case for socialism presented in the 1951-52 *BRS*, but adds a number of points of which the most significant are a simple explanation of capitalist exploitation which rests on the extraction of surplus value, a refutation of the myth that Britain has become a "welfare state," a longer paragraph on women and the family, and a reminder that our biggest asset is the British working class. The second chapter, "How to achieve Socialism," declares that "a transition to socialism without armed conflict is possible today in many countries" thanks to the fact that "more than a third of the world's population has already taken the socialist road". This does not mean that the transition will be smooth and easy. On the contrary, it will take place against a background of "mounting class struggle."

The third chapter, "The Way Forward," assesses the left forces in Britain, and while criticising right-wing trends in the Labour Party, solemnly pledges that Communists will always work for a Labour government as against the Tories. This chapter also mentions the main issues around which a united fight is needed, and on the issue of peace it asserts the CPGB's willingness to work with all peace-loving bodies and people, irrespective of ideological differences.

The fourth and longest chapter, "The Programme of a Socialist Government," deals with nationalisation, planning, the co-operatives, foreign trade and foreign policy, the socialist Budget, independence for the colonies, and social and cultural advances. An entirely new section is devoted to socialist democracy which, it is emphasised, involves trusting the people and avoiding bureaucratic distortions.

The last chapter, "The Communist Party and the Labour Movement," begins by mentioning the CPGB's unique qualities (Marxism, working-class roots, democratic centralism, and the *Daily Worker*), and then goes on to demand the end of all bans and proscriptions against Communists. This should be the prelude to greater unity, including the CPGB's affiliation to the Labour Party, and eventually, the formation of a single working-class party.

8 The 1958-68 decade

During the 1958-68 decade the CPGB was affected by important developments in the international Communist movement and by events at home. The first major development in the international Communist movement was the emergence of Maoism, the new line put forward by the leaders of the Chinese Communist Party (CPC) shortly after the 20th CPSU congress.

This new line included a partial rehabilitation of Stalin, the view that war was inevitable as long as capitalism had not been completely destroyed, the rejection of peaceful transition to socialism as an illusion, and the assertion that the real revolutionary forces were the poor peasant nations rather than the USSR and the working class in industrialised capitalist countries.

In conjunction with a majority of CPs, the CPGB condemned Maoism as a new variant of ultra-leftism, and in 1964 John Gollan, Pollitt's successor as general secretary, published a detailed refutation of the CPC line entitled *Which Road?* As for the few Maoists inside the CPGB, after being defeated at the 1963 party congress by 436 votes to 4, they formed their own party or rather parties, each one vying with one another as to which was more "revolutionary".

The second major development was the military intervention in Czechoslovakia in August 1968 by five Warsaw Pact countries led by the Soviet Union. This was justified by Soviet leaders on the grounds that the Czech Communist Party (CPCz), after rightly getting rid of its Stalinist leadership, had gone too far in the liberalisation process which ensued and that, as a consequence, a counter-revolution was imminent. This time, the Soviet action was not endorsed by all CPs, a number of which (including the CPGB) argued that military intervention was indefensible because the CPCz and the Czechoslovak people were strong enough to defeat the enemies of so-cialism without outside help. On 24 August, three days after the military intervention, the EC of the CPGB issued a strong protest and spoke of a "tragic error." However, in the October 1968 issue of *Labour Monthly*, Palme Dutt took a different position. While agreeing that the CPGB criticisms of the CPSU were "weighty," he proceeded to justify the intervention in a roundabout way, prefacing his remarks with: "It may well be that a future historical judgement ... may reach the conclusion that ...[27]

In spite of Dutt's prestige and the opposition of a few others, the EC's po-sition was endorsed by a majority of the party at the 1968 district congresses and the 1969 national congress, but support was far from being unanimous. The membership was deeply divided on this issue (it still is to this day), but there were no mass resignations as in 1956-58 after Hungary.

Turning now to internal developments, there were both negative and positive features for the CPGB in 1958-68. The main weakness, from which all others stemmed, was a stationary membership around the 30,000 mark.[28] There were objective and subjective reasons for this state of affairs. The ob-jective ones included the cold-war legacy; the unique character of the La-bour Party as the mass party of the working class, organically linked to the trade unions; the two-party system which prevails in this country and makes it very difficult for a third party to establish itself as a credible politi-cal force; and, inevitably, the lingering influence of the past.

Among the subjective factors, the most important were the periodic emergence of dogmatism and revisionism (both feeding each other) and the general lack of clarity about the CP's distinctive role. In the aftermath of de-Stalinisation, revisionism was almost unavoidable, for it invariably gets a new lease of life in the revolutionary movement every time that a crisis makes it imperative to reassess all principles and all values; the tendency is then to discard everything that belongs to the past, the good as well as the bad. The spread of revisionism could have been checked by systematic, regular Marxist education by party members, but this side of party life was sadly neglected. Older members were not encouraged to develop Marx-ist theory and adapt it to the new conditions which had arisen, whereas newcomers were seldom given a solid grounding in the basic principles of Marxism-Leninism.

The membership position was even worse in the Young Communist League (YCL), the autonomous body closely linked to the party whose task is to work among the youth.

One might have thought that the non-conformist and anti-establishment mood of the Sixties would have sent thousands of young people to swell the ranks of the YCL. This, however, did not happen to any appreciable extent, for it was mostly the CND and the ultra-left organisations which were able to register significant membership increases. With regard to the broadly based CND, there should have been no contradiction between belonging to it and being in addition a member of a revolutionary party fighting against the ruling class on all issues instead of just one, crucial though it certainly was. Unfortunately, support for the CND was at first half-hearted on the part of the CPGB and the YCL. When this mistaken approach as corrected, which happened fairly quickly, the poor state of Marxist education prevented many Communists from tackling their work in the peace movement in a principled way, ie by rejecting both sectarian isolation and wishy-washy liberalism.

As for the ultra-left organisations (anarchists, Trotskyists and Maoists) they owed their temporary appeal to the same factors which had helped to revive revisionism, for all periods of crisis and instability foster the parallel growth of revisionist defeatism and ultra-left impatience. Moreover, the events of May-June 1968 in France were a godsend for the ultra-left, because a superficial and tendentious reading of these events (encouraged by the bourgeois media) suggested that the real revolutionaries were those who were throwing paving stones at the police and were destroying property, not the Communists and the trade unionists who stressed the need for an organised and united fight against Gaullism.

A second weakness of the CPGB (a long-standing one) was its failure to become a significant electoral force, as many workers who agreed with its policies were reluctant to let the Tories in by not returning Labour candidates. Finally, the CPGB's failure to achieve any form of unity with the Labour Party was its third major weakness, although most of the bans and proscriptions against Communists were gradually removed thanks to LP-CP grassroots co-operation.

On the positive side, one must mention, first, the party's sheer survival in spite of repeated forecasts of its imminent demise. The survival of the *Daily Worker* was no less of an achievement and could not have happened without the hard work and dedication of thousands of Communists. The paper continued to be the "miracle of Fleet Street"[29] after it changed its name to the *Morning Star* in 1966 (on the dubious ground that the word "worker" was too restrictive).

A second CPGB strength for the period under review was that the party maintained and extended its industrial influence, despite a major setback in 1961 when the Communist leaders of the ETU were found guilty of ballot-rigging, a practice strongly condemned by the EC.

The CPGB was the leading force behind the Liaison Committee for the Defence of Trade Unions. The November 1968 conference called by the Committee was so widely supported that the venue had to be changed twice in order to find a hall big enough to accommodate all the delegates. A day of industrial action was called for 8 November and over 1 million workers responded.

Thirdly, one must mention the countless national and international campaigns initiated or supported by the CPGB over a variety of issues, includ-

ing women's liberation, fight against the EEC, struggle against the multinational firms, and solidarity with Vietnam.

Finally, during the 1958-68 decade the CPGB remained the only political organisation in Britain in which socialist consciousness was kept fully alive thanks to its issuing of books and pamphlets and its holding of educational meetings. The climax of this process was the publication in October 1968 of a new version of the *BRS*.

The 1968 *BRS* does not represent a new CPGB strategy but the updating of the existing one in the light of the fight against Maoism, the events in Czechoslovakia, and the changing situation in Britain. After a short "Introduction," which includes the statement that the CP has a vital role to play but does not seek a position of exclusive leadership, there are five chapters.

The first one, "Britain needs socialism" contains an indictment of state-monopoly capitalism, an analysis of Britain's crisis, and the assertion that "the only path of advance is towards socialism".

The second chapter, "The Communist Party and the Labour Movement," attacks the theory and practice and reformism and offers the revolutionary Communist Party, not as an alternative to Labour, but as a force which can help to transform the LP and provide leadership and inspiration to the whole movement.

The third chapter, "Next Steps Ahead," examines the immediate issues around which a united struggle against state-monopoly capitalism can be waged-defence of living standards, campaigns for public ownership and industrial democracy, the struggle for peace and national independence, the defence and extension of democratic rights, national rights (for Scotland and Wales) and social rights.

The fourth chapter, "Building a Socialist Society," declares that the building of socialism must be preceded by a revolution, ie the winning of political power by the working class and its allies, and that in Britain such a revolution can take place by peaceful means. The same chapter lists the main tasks of a socialist government – nationalisation, planning, democratisation and a peaceful foreign policy. A special section on socialist democracy commits the CPGB to pluralism and describes what is meant by the transformation of Parliament. The section on the LP and the CP envisages the co-operation of the two working-class parties.

In the last chapter, "The Choice Is Ours," the 1968 *BRS* states that socialism is to be built by the people themselves, not just for them; that the existing socialist countries show that socialism works; that these same countries, however, provide an inspiration, not a model; and finally, that socialism is the first stage towards a higher society, a communist society.

The chief novelties of the 1968 *BRS* concern the peaceful transition to socialism, pluralism, Parliament and the CPGB's attitude to the Labour Party. The first topic had been one of the main issues in the polemic against Maoism. The 1968 *BRS* stresses that "peaceful" simply means "without civil war" and certainly not a smooth path without struggle. It further asserts that a peaceful revolution is not a certainty but a realistic possibility provided the working class is strong and provided the building of a broad popular alliance is accompanied by political education. With regard to pluralism, it was implied in the 1958 *BRS*, whereas in the aftermath of Czechoslovakia, the CPGB decided to be absolutely clear on this issue, so that the 1968 *BRS* states for the first time that "parties hostile to socialism" will be allowed provided they respect the law. Such a commitment was rejected by a substantial number of party members and still is to this day, although it is worth noting that support for pluralism is not the prerogative of Euro-communists. On Parliament, the 1968 *BRS* advocates a fairer electoral system, a single chamber, and accountability of the government to the House and of the MPs themselves to the people. Lastly, with regard to the LP, what is new in the 1968 *BRS* is the statement, never made before in a CPGB programme, that the Communist Party does not seek to replace the Labour Party, but rather to work with it both before and after the socialist revolution.

9 The 1968-78 decade

During the 1968-78 period the CPGB's membership and electoral influence continued to decline, but on the other hand, its militant industrial work and impact were still considerable. Party membership went down from 30,607 in June 1969 to 25,300 in August 1977. In parliamentary elections, whereas the 57 CPGB candidates totalled 62,000 votes in 1966 (an average of 1,089 votes per candidate), in 1974, the 44 Communist candidates totalled 32,773 votes (an average of 774 per candidate). The position was very slightly better in local elections. For example, in 1973, the 608 CPGB candidates totalled 165,743 votes, and 23 of them were elected, 13 in Scotland, 6 in Wales, and 4 in England.

In the industrial field, the first development which must be mentioned was the party's involvement in the struggle against the anti-union Industrial Relations Act which was passed in 1970. The Liaison Committee called for a one-day strike against the Act, and 3 million workers responded. When the Act was invoked against five leaders of the London dockers (including Bernie Steer, a Communist, and Vic Turner, who joined later), the government had to yield to public protest and the five were quickly released from Pentonville Prison on the 26th June 1972). Shortly afterwards, Communists were again in the lead when the Upper Clyde workers occupied their shipyard to stop it from being closed down. The best-known leaders were three Communists, Jimmy Reid, who later joined the Labour Party, Jimmy Airlie and Sam Barr. The struggle lasted 18 months and resulted in victory.

One must also mention the strike of building workers in 1972, which led to the arrest of 24 pickets and their trial at Shrewsbury in 1973. The political nature of the trial was illustrated by the fact that the defendants were charged with "conspiracy," the latter loose term covering any attempt on the part of strikers to act in an organised and collective way.

The Communist Des Warren was given the harshest sentence and was sent to prison for three years, while his co-worker, Eric (Ricky) Tomlinson, got two years. Both had firmly rejected the charge of conspiracy against them and had counter-attacked by saying that there was indeed a conspiracy – a conspiracy between the Tory government and the employers against the working people. The campaign to secure the release of the Shrewsbury 2 – as they became known-lasted a long time but was not successful.

The biggest industrial strikes of the period under review were the miners' strike in 1972 (involving flying pickets) and in 1973, The then Prime Minister Edward Heath tried to run industry on a three-day week, but the public were on the side of the miners. The Tory government then, forced a general election in February 1974, which was won by Labour. Although the contest was ostensibly between Tories and Labour, it was the Communist Party, and especially Mick McGahey, the Communist president of the NUM in Scotland, who were most bitterly attacked by Heath and his colleagues. And with good cause since it was above all the CPGB's factory branches which had organised solidarity actions in support of the miners.

In November 1977, the CPGB held its 35th congress, at which a revised version of the BRS was adopted. This was published in 1978. It is worth pointing to its chief novelties, in the order which they occur in the document rather than in order of importance. The first one may be found in a section of the first chapter, entitled "How capitalist rule is maintained."

Unlike previous versions of the BRS, the 1978 version does not describe capitalist rule as being mainly coercive, but stresses that it relies mainly on consent. In order to turn its victims into willing victims, the capitalist class has concluded a practical alliance with other social strata. As we shall see presently, the 1978 BRS drew the conclusion that such a capitalist-dominated alliance had to be replaced by a popular alliance led by the working class.

The second novelty of the 1978 BRS lay in its detailed analysis of class forces in modem Britain. The main contending classes were said to be the working class (broadly defined as including all those who sell their labour power in order to live) and the capitalist class, whilst the intermediate strata fluctuate between the two, but can be won over to support the labour movement against the monopolists.

The third novelty was the concept of the "broad democratic alliance," which now replaced the "anti-monopoly alliance" of the 1968 BRS. The Euro-communist interpretation that the change represented giving up a "narrow" class approach was not borne out by the text itself which repeatedly stressed that the leading force in the alliance was the working class and that the main enemy were the monopolists.

The fourth novelty of the 1978 BRS was that it includes a longer section on the Communist Party, listing its five essential characteristics, viz a Marxist-Leninist outlook, working-class roots, democratic structure, discipline in carrying out majority decisions, and internationalism. The *BRS* stresses that the CPGB must become a "mass party," not only by greatly increasing its membership, but by its ability to draw more and more people into political action.

The fifth novelty was the special attention paid to the various movements which have arisen in recent years, the women's movement, the black movement and the struggle against racism, the national movement in Scotland and Wales, the ecology movement, the movements connected with the problems of local communities, the peace movement, the youth movement, and the pensioners' movement.

The *BRS* acknowledged the importance of these "new social forces," but warns that none of them can win its demands on its own. What is needed is "Alliance – not isolation" (p33).

The sixth novelty was what the 1978 *BRS* added to the issue of the peaceful road to socialism. In the light of the tragic Chilean experience, it did not rule out the possibility of a right-wing armed coup against a left government, but rather discusses it in a serious way, examining both how it can be prevented and the need to suppress it by force if it takes place at all. It paid great attention to the role of the armed forces and the police, saying that a non-violent revolution is impossible unless these are neutralised, if not actually won over to the cause of a united labour movement.

The seventh novelty was the distinction between the transitional period (Chapter Three) and the period of building socialism proper (Chapter Four). Such a distinction does not mean that the CPGB's strategy regards various stages as separate from one another, but rather that the socialist revolution is a continuous process.

The final novelty concerned the Labour Party. For the first time, a CPGB programme did not speak of a single working-class party, but envisaged instead lasting co-operation as well as healthy competition between the LP and the CP.

10 The rise of Euro-communism (1979-86)

For the CPGB the recent period is unfortunately characterised by a steady decline in its membership and influence and by the emergence of Euro-communism. (It is perfectly legitimate to see a relationship of cause and effect between the two aspects.)

The membership dropped to about 20,000 in 1980 and reached an all-time low of about 11,000 in 1985.[30] The party's electoral significance continues to be derisory, but whereas in the past this was compensated by industrial influence, the number of factory branches has been dwindling and the party's involvement in industrial struggles has been consistently discouraged or watered down by a leadership which came increasingly under the domination of Euro-communism.

What exactly is Euro-communism? The phrase itself was coined by the capitalist media in the mid-Seventies to describe the evolution of some western CPs, mainly the Italian (PCI) and the Spanish (PCE) parties. In 1977, the Spanish leader Santiago Carillo endorsed the label and published a book to describe what it involved.[31]

Broadly speaking, Euro-communism represents the complete rejection of the Soviet experience, the criticism of existing socialist countries as undemocratic and not even socialist, a greater stress on the vague concept of "people" rather than on the working class, and the view that socialism is the extension of capitalist democracy rather than its abolition and transformation.

In Britain, Euro-communism was eagerly adopted by a faction which won control of *Marxism Today*, the party's monthly organ. It secured a major victory at the 39th (Special) congress of the CPGB by becoming the majority group on the new EC.

On the other hand, it suffered a resounding defeat at successive AGMs of the PPPS (People's Press Printing Society), the co-operative which runs the *Morning Star*: in 1984, and again in 1985 and in 1986, the great majority of shareholders (most of them CPGB members) expressed their confidence in the management committee and the editors of the paper, rejecting the EC criticism that the *Star* had become narrow and sectarian.

The Euro-communist leadership severed all links with the paper and, in contravention of the party rules, instructed members not to help with its circulation. The Euro-communist leadership also started a series of disciplinary measures (including expulsions and suspensions) against genuine Marxist-Leninists.

It was against this background that the Communist Campaign Group (CCG) was formed in 1985, not as a faction but as an organisation whose sole aims were the reinstatement of expelled comrades and the restoration of the party to its Marxist-Leninist basis.

NOTES

1 George Tate and AL Morton, *The British Labour Movement 1770-1920* (Lawrence and Wishart, 1962), p99.
2 A particularly informative study is G Tate and AL Morton, op. cit.
3 Harry Pollitt, *Looking Ahead* (The Communist Party, 1947), pp 41-2.
4 See in particular James Klugmann, *History of the Communist Party of Great Britain*, vol 1 (Lawrence and Wishart, 1968), and James Klugmann's article in *Marxism Today* Ganuary 1960).
5 See Lenin, *'Left-wing Communism', an infantile disorder*, in which chapter 9 is devoted to the refutation of the views then held by Sylvia Pankhurst and William Gallacher. Gallacher was eventually won over by Lenin's arguments, but not Sylvia Pankhurst.
6 See James Klugmann, op. cit.. (2 vols.), and Noreen Branson, *History of the Communist Party of Great Britain* 1927-41 (Lawrence and Wishart, 1985).
7 For further details, see Noreen Branson, op.cit., pp4, 26, 31-4, and 150-7. See also George Matthews, "The quest for unity" (article in *Comment*, 7 February 1981).
8 "Social-democratic" was the label applied by Communists to all the parties of the Second or Labour International because it was the actual name adopted by the German party, the strongest party in the LSI at that time.
9 For further details, see Noreen Branson, op. cit. ch.9 (pp58-73) and Idris Cox's article in *Marxism Today*, October 1970.
10 See N Branson, op. cit., p108 and p246.
11 For further details, see Peter Kerrigan's article in *Marxism Today*, December 1970.
12 For further details about the birth and early years of the *Daily Worker*, see N Branson, op. cit., pp52-7.
13 Initially, the name of the basic party unit in the CPGB, as in continental CPs, was "cell," a word chosen to stress the fact that each unit was part of a living body. Later, it was decided to use a more traditional British terminology. The process started in 1936 (see N Branson, op. cit., pp173-4), and by 1943, all basic units were known as "branches," the "Central Committee" as the "Executive Committee," and the "Political Bureau" as the "Political Committee."
14 For further details, see N Branson, op. cit., pp45-6.
15 The expression had first been used by Stalin in a 1924 article (see Stalin, *Works*, vol. 6, Moscow 1953, p294).
16 Even when the seventh Comintern congress adopted the Popular Front strategy it did not formally repudiate the "Class against Class" line. It merely said that a new situation demanded a new approach. At that time it was unthinkable that a policy which had been associated with the "great Stalin" could have been pronounced wrong.

17 Quoted in John Mahon, *Harry Pollitt* (Lawrence and Wishart, 1976), p235.
18 For a fuller account of these activities, see N Branson, op. cit., especially chapters 9, 12, 16 and 18.
19 RP Dutt, *Turning Point of the World* (Summer 1941 pamphlet), p9.
20 See the proceedings of a conference held in April 1979 in John Attfield and Stephen Williams (ed), *1939: The Communist Party of Great Britain and the War* (Lawrence and Wishart, 1984).
21 Harry Pollitt, quoted in John Mahon, op.cit., p269.
22 EC's comment on the draft revised text of the *BRS* (CP, 1957), p iv.
23 Draft revised text of the *BRS* (CP, 1957), p12.
24 ibid.
25 *World News*, 18 May 1957, p316.
26 *Report of the Commission on Inner-Party Democracy* (CP, 1957), p46.
27 R Palme Dutt, in *Labour Monthly* (October, 1968), p456.
28 CPGB membership figures for the period under review are as follows:

    1958: 24,670
    1960: 26,052
    1961: 27,541
    1962: 32,492
    1963: 33,008
    1964: 34,281
    1965: 35,589
    1966: 32,708
    1967: 32,562

29 The expression was first applied by Lord Northcliffe to the survival of the then militant *Daily Herald*. It is even more appropriate to the *Morning Star*, the one daily paper in Britain which is not owned and controlled by millionaires.
30 Membership figures for the 1980-86 period are as follows:

    1980: 19,723
    1981: 18,458
    1982: 16,520
    1983: 15,691
    1984: No figures
    1985: 12,711
    1986: 10,999

31 Santiago Carillo's book, *"Eurocommunism" and the State*, was translated into English and published by Lawrence and Wishart in 1977.

Brief note on the Internationals
First International: International Working Men's Association (IWMA) (1864-76)

Second International: Labour and Socialist International (LSI) (1889-)

Third International: Communist International (CI or Comintern) (1919-1943).

PART 2

Analytical Introduction

The role of the Communist Party

The Communist Party was founded in 1920. For most of its existence the Communist Party has been an integral part of the British labour movement and its influence on the theory and practice of socialism in Britain has been considerably greater than its small numbers would suggest. Yet, it is widely believed, even by friendly critics, that there is no room for such a party in a country like ours. It may suit the Russians or the Cubans, perhaps even the Italians or the French, but it is, at best, an anomaly in Britain. For example, in 1956, Sydney Silverman, who was then a member of the Labour Party executive, conceded that: "if a country is building Socialism by Communist paths ... there is no need and no use for a Social-Democratic party" in that country, but he went on to say that:

> in a country where, by tradition, by history, by social organisation, for any other reason, the road to Socialism must necessarily be the social-democratic road, there is equally no need and no use for a Communist party. Certainly there is no need or use of such a party in Great Britain.[1]

The crux of the matter, however, is whether it is indeed true that in Britain the road to socialism "must necessarily be the social-democratic road". One cannot deny that both "tradition" and "history" account for the appeal of such a road in this country, but Silverman failed to provide the historical reasons which led to such a situation. The difference between social-democracy and communism is the difference between reformism and revolution, and before analysing the reasons which account for the greater impact of the former over the latter in Britain, the essential characteristics of each approach must be briefly described.

Reformism is not a well-defined theory, it is rather a form of political behaviour which assumes that the present social system can be modified and improved by a series of reforms and does not have to be abolished altogether. Moreover, as the reforms envisaged can be jointly implemented by workers' and capitalists' representatives, reformism is inseparable from "class collaboration", ie from the attempt to recognise and harmonise the conflicting interests of the capitalists, who live off other people's labour, and of the workers, who sell their labour power to the owners of the means of production) Reformism is not just the belief that reforms are needed to alleviate social injustice – all sensible people would agree with that – but the assumption that by themselves reforms can solve the problems of modern society and that the capitalist system can go on forever, provided it is modified from time to time.

It is unlikely that members of the Labour Party would admit that reformism, as defined above, is their basic political philosophy. This is why is it is important to look at what the Labour Party does, either when it is in office or in opposition. Experience shows that it bases its policy on "managing" capitalism rather than on making inroads into the capitalists' wealth and power; at times, some of its representatives have even boasted that they are better managers of capitalism than the Tories.

Revolutionaries, on the other hand, believe that the capitalist system is based on a number of irreconcilable contradictions, such as the permanent clash between the social character of production and the private character of ownership and control, the fundamental opposition between the employers' interests (to make profits) and the workers' interests (to own collectively the wealth they produce), and that because every advance for the workers must conflict with the interests of the capitalists, this irreconcilable contradiction underlines why improving the system cannot solve its structural crisis: it must be abolished and replaced by a system under which the means of production are socially owned and controlled, the satisfaction of people's needs becomes the prime incentive of the national economy, and state power is in the hands of the working people.

A couple of examples will illustrate the difference between the reformist and the revolutionary attitude. The first one concerns the struggle for wage rises. Both reformists and revolutionaries may be united in this struggle (though reformists often assert that wage rises are wrong because they cause inflation), but they view its significance in different ways. For reformists, the winning of a wage rise is an isolated economic victory, whereas for revolutionaries it represents not only economic advance, but a political step in the struggle to abolish the wage system itself.

The other example concerns nationalisation. In 1945, the Labour government nationalised coal and the railways, but, first, it did not appoint work-ers to run these industries, on the grounds, presumably, that only members of the ruling elite make good administrators, and secondly, it left the rest of industry (about 80%) in private hands. As for the revolutionary Communist Party, it welcomed the nationalisation of coal and the rail ways, but it fought for workers' representation on the boards of nationalised industries, and furthermore, it did not regard the so-called "mixed economy" as a substi-tute for socialism, but rather as a stepping stone toward it. Incidentally, this does not necessarily mean that in the socialist Britain envisaged by Com-munists there will be no private sector, it simply means that small firms would continue to exist, provided they were integrated within a national plan. This is in fact what all Communist Party programmes have advocated from 1935 onwards.

The long-standing debate between reformists and revolutionaries has recently acquired a new, almost ironic aspect inasmuch as the fight for re-forms in contemporary Britain is itself a revolutionary fight. In the past, the British ruling class could afford, albeit reluctantly, to accept reforms and make concessions to its working class, largely because a great part of its profits came from the exploitation of a vast colonial empire. Now, the em-pire has virtually gone, and in addition, other capitalist powers, the USA, Germany and Japan in the first place, have ousted Britain from its former dominant world position.

As a result, British imperialism is in deep crisis, the deepest in its history, and it can no longer tolerate reforms, especially structural reforms such as partial nationalisation or progressive decentralisation. Instead, it has em-barked on a policy of confrontation with the labour movement and with all democratic forces. In order to resist this ruling-class offensive, a revolu-tionary party is needed more than ever. For it alone can provide a scientific analysis of the crisis, inspire and co-ordinate the mass movements which arise and are bound to arise, and offer a realistic way out of the crisis, the socialist road.

If, as Communists believe, a revolutionary party is an objective neces-sity in Britain, how do they account for the fact that the opposite view is widely held and that reformism has for so long dominated the thinking of the labour movement? The most important reason is that Britain became the classic land of reformism because it was the land where capitalism, and then imperialism, "the highest form of capitalism" (Lenin), first came into being, thus giving the British ruling class considerable room for manoeuvre in tak-ing on Labour leaders as junior partners. At the end of the last century and at the beginning of the present one, British workers believed in reformism because it seemed to work: democratic freedoms were gained, by struggle, and living standards were improved, again by struggle. When revolutionar-ies argued that all these gains were limited, representing only a small frac-tion of what could be achieved under a system of social ownership and planned production for use, they were often dismissed as utopian dreamers. When they further argued that under capital ism all gains were precarious and could be eroded, if not abolished, by a ruling class in the throes of a deep crisis, they were again largely dis missed, this time as prophets of doom. In today's Britain, the revolutionary case can no longer be ignored, as fact after fact, hardship after hardship, consistently demonstrate its validity.

And yet, there has been no automatic massive switch from the ideology of reformism to that of revolutionary struggle. Marxists have never been so naive as to expect that such a switch would occur as soon as conditions became worse. They never subscribed to the view that bad conditions immediately give rise to the will and determination to fight them, first, because, they know that it takes time to give up long-entrenched ideas and practices, and secondly, because they realise that wrong ideas will linger on "until they are driven out, in bitter struggle, in the battle of ideas, by the idea of Socialism, of Marxism-Leninism", as Harry Pollitt put it in 1952.[2]

In order to wage this battle, a revolutionary party, a party whose programme and organisation are based on the class struggle, has a crucial role to play. The left in the Labour Party now realises that reformist policies have had their day and that new ones are needed. Communists welcome this growing realisation as well as its practical manifestations. They do not say that they alone can lead the British people along the revolutionary road, but they do say- and their entire history substantiates their claim – that:

> The vital need is for an organisation of socialists, guided by the principles of scientific socialism, everywhere among the people, in all the struggles, in all the unions, in all the progressive movements, and able to give leadership to them – in other words, an organised party, as distinct from the left groups in the Labour Party, the separate unions and the other social forces and movements. It was to fulfil this role that the Communist Party was founded in 1920 by Marxists in the labour movement.[3]

One of the key features of the Communist Party, which can be found in all the programmes, is the fact that it bases its entire policy on the science of Marxism-Leninism. This represents a significant novelty in British politics. Before 1920, all major parties in this country prided themselves on being, in true British fashion, essentially pragmatic and down to earth. The Labour Party was no different in this respect, so that it has become a tiring platitude among its leaders and many of its members to boast of being above all "practical".

When the CPGB emerged on the political scene, it was the first party (as distinct from sects and groups) to say that the practical common sense of the British people and of the British working class was indeed a great asset, but that it had to be supplanted by theory, by science, on pain of the movement being forever condemned to groping in the dark and "muddling through" without ever getting anywhere. Despite all the pundits who repeat ad nauseam that contempt for theory is an innate British characteristic, it is in fact something which was – and still is – encouraged by the ruling class and by reformist leaders. The ruling class felt that it did not need ideas since it had for a long time been chosen by God to preside over the destinies of an empire on which the sun never sets. The reformist leaders shun theory on the ground that it is a pastime for intellectuals whereas all that the workers need to do is to elect the "right" (in every sense of the word!) MPs and union bosses and leave it all to them. Communists believe that the working people need ideas because, in the words of Marx, "ideas become a material force when they grip the masses". This is why every Communist Party programme has been based on Marxism, the revolutionary theory of the working class.

Consistent features of Communist strategy

In the following pages, we shall examine in some detail the key issues dealt with by successive Communist Party programmes and we shall see the various changes which have taken place over the years. Before such a study of the party's evolution is undertaken, it is useful to keep in mind what all the programmes have in common, from *FSB* to the *BRS*.

The first consistent feature is the class approach, ie the understanding that politics can be treated as a science only when it is based on the principle proclaimed at the beginning of the 1848 Manifesto of the Communist Party that: "The history of all hitherto existing societies has been the history of class struggles." The forms in which the class struggle has to be waged are bound to vary but its essence is governed by three constant principles – in order to win, the working class must be united; it must lead other social strata; and it must isolate the main enemy.

The second consistent feature is the indictment of capitalism and the assertion that such a system must be abolished and replaced with social ism. This is not presented as some kind of dogma in which the faithful must believe, but it is always accompanied by a detailed analysis of Britain's problems at the time of writing and by a rational demonstration that socialism alone can open up a better future, free from poverty, war, unemployment and cultural decline.

On one issue in particular, all the programmes show the superiority of socialism over capitalism, and that is the issue of democracy. First, they remind us that the democratic rights enjoyed by the British people were never given to them by allegedly enlightened rulers but had to be fought for; so long as capitalism exists, these rights are precarious: they can be eroded and even destroyed unless the people are vigilant. Secondly, all the programmes express their confidence that socialist democracy is the only genuine democracy because it has a solid material basis (the people's ownership of the means of production), a firm political basis (control of the state and other institutions by the working class and its allies), and a strong ideological basis (the values of co-operation instead of those of the rat race).

In *FSB* (in conformity with the terminology and beliefs of the time), we find that "workers' dictatorship means democracy for the workers," ie that the suppression of an exploiting class results in an extension of democracy for working people. And in the 1978 edition of the *BRS*, we are told that democracy means people's control and that "socialism alone makes such popular control possible" (p58). Thirdly, in all the programmes, democracy is not just the aim of the movement but the method it uses in order to achieve its aim. In other words, what is stressed throughout is that it is not a small group of dedicated revolutionaries which can bring about funda mental social change but the broad masses of the people.

A third consistent feature is that the strategy of the Communist Party is a revolutionary strategy, in the sense that its goal is the abolition of capitalist property relations and the transfer of power from the capitalist class to the working class and its allies. It is true that the party's views concerning the forms of the revolution have changed considerably (belief in violent revolution before the war and in a peaceful transition to socialism from 1951 onwards), but such an evolution, dictated by changed circumstances, has never affected the party's firm adherence to the essence of the revolution. From *FSB* to the 1978 *BRS* the guiding thought is that the final victory of socialism depends, not on piecemeal adjustments to the existing system, but on the winning of power by the working people. On this, the 1978 *BRS* expresses the view, which has been that of the Communist Party throughout its entire history, when it says that:

> ...to achieve socialism the working class and its allies must take political, economic and state power out of the hands of the capitalist class. (p3)

A fourth consistent feature is internationalism. Ever since Marx and Engels issued their clarion call in 1848, "Workers of all lands, unite!", international working-class solidarity has been one of the cornerstones of Communist policy. In practice, it has involved and still involves three things. In the first place, supporting the workers' struggles against capitalism everywhere, because in the modem era the class struggle is international. Just as the capitalists of all countries give one another assistance when the "sacred" profit system is threatened (which does not preclude fierce competition), so the workers of all countries must assist one another in the fight against their common enemy.

A vivid example of the international character of the class struggle was provided in 1917-18, when on the one hand, 14 capitalist powers (some of which were still at war with each other) united in an attempt to destroy the new socialist republic in Russia and, on the other hand, when that same republic was defended by the actions of the world working class, such as the "Hands Off Russia" committees which spread throughout Britain and the refusal of the London dockers to load the "Jolly George" with arms and munitions which were intended for use against the Soviet revolution.

In the second place, for British Communists, internationalism has involved the struggle against British imperialism before the war and British neo-colonialism after the war. Once again, a comparison is revealing. *FSB* proclaims "the right of all countries now forming part of the British Empire to complete self-determination up to and including complete separation". The 1978 *BRS*, for its part asserts:

> Independence should be granted to all remaining British colonies ... Active support should be given to national-liberation struggles ... Britain should repudiate neo-colonialist policies... (p43)

Finally, internationalism involves supporting the countries where Communists are in power and are building socialism. Before the war, there was only one such country – the Soviet Union – and support for the first land of socialism was part and parcel of the *FSB*, especially since the USSR set an example to the rest of the world by proving that socialism works. After the war, CPGB programmes spoke, first, of supporting the Soviet Union as well as the new people's democracies, and eventually, of solidarity with "the socialist countries".

There is no doubt that the uncritical, unconditional support of the Stalin era has been replaced with an attitude of critical support which does not hide some of the faults and limitations in existing socialist countries, but the emphasis remains – rightly – on the positive aspect, as can be seen from the following paragraph in the 1978 *BRS*, which deserves to be quoted in full:

> The economic, social, political and cultural advances of the socialist countries have shown socialism's great potential for human development despite the problems which exist within these countries and in relations between them. In the post-war period the Soviet Union and other socialist states have achieved consistent economic growth increases and maintained full employment and stable prices, in contrast to the crisis-ridden economies of the US and capitalist Western Europe, showing that capitalism will eventually be outpaced by socialism. (p11)

The last consistent feature is the stress on the crucial role of the Communist Party. Initially, it was seen as the only one which could provide leadership, and the 1935 *FSB* described it as the "General Staff" of the working class in its war against capitalism. Subsequent programmes, beginning with the 1939 DP, have increasingly recognised the part which can be played by other forces in the struggle for socialism, especially the Labour Party, but until 1968 the hope continued to be expressed that a single working-class party would eventually be formed in Britain. Such an approach is no longer that of the 1978 *BRS*, and even in its 1968 predecessor the prospect of a "single Marxist party" was seen as belonging to the distant future.

We shall discuss the matter in greater detail in Chapter 5. What is worth noting at this stage is the remarkable similarity among all the Communist Party programmes on what constitutes the distinctive features of the Communist Party, viz its Marxist-Leninist basis and outlook, its working-class roots, its democratic-centralist organisation, and its internationalism.

NOTES

1 Sydney Silverman, in *Labour Monthly*, December 1956.
2 Harry Pollitt, *Britain Arise* (CP, 1952), p34.
3 1978 *BRS*, p25

1

The Programme in Politics

In this first chapter of our analysis, it is proposed to examine the general ways in which a Communist programme differs from the programmes of all other political parties. We are concerned at this stage with the fundamental difference with regard to content, ie with the fact that everything put forward in a programme issued by the Communist Party is meant to contribute to the achievement and the building of a socialist society (an aim which, it might be argued, the CP shares with other left organisations). The purpose of this chapter is rather to focus on another set of differences, all of which hinge on the nature of the programme, on the role it is expected to play in politics.

Let us begin with the differences which show what a CPGB programme is not. It is not an election manifesto, it is not an official statement nor a congress resolution on a number of topical issues, and it is not a list of measures which a progressive government (with or without Communists) is expected to carry out.

The reason why a Communist Party programme is not an election manifesto is that elections, whether local or parliamentary, take place at regular intervals which are fixed by custom but do not correspond to new phases in social and political development. Moreover, what all parties apart from the CP tend to do before an election is to promise the voters the implementation of some policies, an implementation which depends exclusively on whether the party in question is returned to power.

The Communist concept of politics, on the other hand, does not regard the people's involvement as coming to an end when a vote has been taken. The vote is only one step. It should be preceded and followed by mass struggles outside Parliament. Without a combination of parliamentary and extra-parliamentary actions, there can be no radical social changes.

The reason why a Communist Party programme is not an official statement put out by the leadership or a resolution adopted at a two-yearly congress derives from the fact that for Communists a party programme is a long-term and comprehensive document. This does not mean that Executive Committee statements and congress resolutions do not matter. All it means is that they do not and cannot commit the party in the same way or to the same extent. One might say that statements and resolutions affect the transient tactics of the party, whereas its programme is the expression of its overall strategy.

Lastly, there are three reasons why a Communist Party programme is not similar to a government programme. The first one concerns the long-term and comprehensive character of the document, which has just been mentioned. The second one is that, so far, the presence of the Communist Party in a British government has been only a remote possibility.

Apart from the pre-war period when the party's goal was the formation of British soviets to rule the country, the perspective envisaged by the post-war editions of the *BRS* has been that of a progressive Labour government, to be followed at some unspecified stage by a socialist government based on a Labour-Communist coalition.

Incidentally, even before the war, the 1939 *DP* called for the formation of an anti-fascist Labour government and consequently included, but only as part of the document as a whole, a list of measures which such a government should implement. By far the most important reason is that Communists draw a sharp distinction between the respective roles of government and party. The former should be accountable to the latter if it is a one-party government, or to a group of parties if the basis is a coalition, but in either case a party's role, especially in the case of a revolutionary party, is much broader than that of a government. The government is only the executive, but for Marxists what matters much more is the participation of the people, of the working class in the first place. It is in order to provide leadership to this participation, to co-ordinate it and give it a sense of direction that the Communist Party exists. Its programme is intended to cover all the issues over which the working class and popular movement must be active and to show the realistic perspectives which can be fought for.

Let us now turn to the four distinctive characteristics of a Communist Party programme, viz its historical analysis of the phase reached by capitalism at the time of publication, its theoretical appraisal of what might be called the mechanics of capitalist rule, its examination of the strategy and tactics of the revolution, and its outline of the main features of socialist society.

The first example of a historical analysis of a given stage of capitalism occurs in the 1929 manifesto, *Class against Class*, which describes modem capitalism as being in deep crisis. From this correct analysis, which was that of the Comintern as a whole, the programme drew the incorrect conclusion that as a result of the crisis all the forces which were not openly revolutionary, the right, the centre, and the reformist left, were the conscious supporters of the capitalist system, whilst the CP was its one and only opponent. Hence the opening sentence in the document:

> The Communist Party is the party of the working class, in fundamental opposition to all other parties. (p5)

Compare this sectarian declaration with what Marx and Engels said in their *Manifesto*, viz: "The Communists do not form a separate party opposed to other working class parties."

Hence also, the necessary conclusion: a policy of "class against class" requires a fight against the Tories, "the party of imperialism;" the Liberals, "also a party of imperialism;" and against the Labour Party, which is "the third capitalist party". Instead of looking forward to a Labour government and helping to elect one, the workers should begin a campaign around the slogan of a "Revolutionary Workers' Government." That such an analysis ignored an urgent need to unite the working class against what was rightly called "the capitalist offensive" does not affect the one point with which we are concerned at this stage, namely, that a Communist programme depends on "the concrete analysis of concrete conditions".

In a later chapter, we shall have more to say about the weaknesses of the 1929 analysis. What cannot be denied is that it represented an attempt to apply Marxism and to draw up a revolutionary strategy accordingly.

For the time being, there is no need to describe in great detail the way in which other Communist Party programmes are also based on a similar attempt to grasp the main features of the then existing situation. Suffice it to mention that the 1935 *FSB* opens with a chapter entitled "The Class Struggle in Britain *Today*" (my emphasis – MA) and that it emphasises the need for a "United Struggle": that the main novelty in the 1939 *DP* is that it draws upon the experience of the anti-fascist struggle and of the Popular Front; that the strategy outlined in the 1951-52 *BRS* makes sense only in the light of the Marxist assessment of the changed balance of class forces after the defeat of Hitler Germany by the wartime coalition of the USA, Great Britain and the USSR; that the 1958 *BRS* reappraises the tasks of Communists in the aftermath of the 20th CPSU congress and the de-Stalinisation process it initiated; that the 1968 *BRS* begins by showing that the short-lived post-war boom has been followed by "a deep-seated crisis of the whole economic, political and social system" which "affects adversely every aspect of life"; and that the 1978 *BRS* extends the analysis of the crisis and of state-monopoly capitalism.

In every one of these cases, the need for a new or revised programme was the result of changes in the objective situation in the previous decade or so.

The second distinctive feature of all Communist Party programmes is that they are based, not only on the kind of historical analysis which has just been examined, but also on a theoretical appraisal of the way in which capitalism works. This aspect is particularly evident in three programmes, the 1939 *DP*, the 1968 *BRS* and the 1978 *BRS*. In the 1939 DP, the first five chapters (out of 10 in all) are devoted to a scientific evaluation of capitalism, as can be seen from their titles: chapter 1 is called "Britain today"; chapter 2,"Capitalism and the class struggle"; chapter 3, "Democracy and the State in Britain"; chapter 4, "The British Empire"; and chapter 5, "Imperialism and the downfall of capitalism."

The first chapter describes the capitalists' domination of all aspects British life; the second one contains a lucid summary of the Marxist theory of surplus value, the capitalist crisis, the class struggle and revolution; the third chapter outlines in simple language the Marxist-Leninist theory of the state and applies it to British conditions; the fourth chapter describes the British Empire as a highly profitable outlet for the capital which the ruling class does not invest in Britain, and shows that those who suffer from colonial exploitation are both the colonies and the British people themselves; the fifth chapter begins with a clear summary of Lenin's analysis of imperialism as the monopoly stage of capitalism, and goes on to give a short historical account of the development of imperialism up to 1939 – the First World War, the general crisis of the system aggravated by the existence of the Soviet Union and the victory of socialism in that country, the menace of fascism as "the terroristic dictatorship of the most reactionary sections of monopoly capital," and the beginning, in everything but name, of the second imperialist war [NB the *DP* was written in August 1939] launched by the fascist powers, aided and abetted by Britain and France.

In the 1968 *BRS*, the first chapter "Britain needs socialism" is at the same time a restatement of the long-standing Marxist analysis of capitalism and a concrete proof of its relevance today.

The chief innovation is the section on "State Monopoly Capitalism" where we are shown, for the first time in a CPGB programme, that today "the capitalist state is intertwined with the great banks and the monopolies".

A little further down the *BRS* points to the main conclusion to be drawn from such a development and says:

> Socialism is the logical way to meet the present need for public finance and planning, for larger industrial units, for growing social services. (p16)

In the first chapter of the 1978 *BRS*, "Why Britain needs socialism," the analysis of capitalism is brought up to date in that it refers to the role of the multinational firms, but the most striking novelty is to be found in the section entitled "How capitalist rule is maintained," which, as we saw earlier, refers to the mixture of coercion and consent which characterises the way in which the capitalist class maintains its rule. Unlike previous programmes, the *BRS* now puts the emphasis on consent, which is achieved thanks to the almost unchallenged domination of capitalist ideas. Not content with exercising a degree of coercion through its economic strength and its control of state institutions, the British bourgeoisie has been able to achieve a temporary ideological consensus, with the result that:

> ...it relies primarily on the fact that millions of people believe that the capitalist system is the natural way to organise society...
> (p9)

Such a victory is due to a number of factors – capitalist control of the media and of cultural institutions like the schools and the universities, alliance between the monopolists and other social strata, the concessions made to working people immediately after the war, and the reformist outlook of the right wing in the Labour Party.

> Thus persuasion, politics and coercion are all utilised by the ruling class to maintain its rule. (p10)

Although this approach is new as far as CPGB programmes are concerned, Eurocommunists are mistaken in their assumption that it is a novelty introduced into Marxism by Gramsci's theories about hegemony which were eagerly seized upon by some Western CPs in the 1970s. As John Hoffman convincingly shows, the idea that capitalism rules by consent as well as by coercion is by no means alien to the classics of Marxism.[1] Marx, Engels and Lenin always looked upon the ideological struggle as crucial, but unlike our modern revisionists, they did not divorce it from other forms of struggle because, as good dialectical materialists, they knew that ideas reflect material conditions, but can, in their turn, influence the battles which are aimed at transforming these conditions. Certainly, bourgeois hegemony must be replaced with working-class hegemony, but this requires waging the battle of ideas as well as conducting, social and political struggle.

Moreover, the merit of the 1978 *BRS* is not simply that it attaches great importance to the battle of ideas, but that it clearly states that the purpose of waging this battle is to win it. It sees the overriding aim as one of overcoming "capitalist ideas... so that the people can develop confidence in their own ability to run society". (p10)

The third distinctive characteristic of all Communist Party programmes is that they are not only concerned with the "why" of the revolution, but with the "how" of it. This does not mean that they aim to provide the movement with a kind of "Handbook for Revolutionaries", but rather that they boldly face the practical problems which are bound to arise, the pitfalls to avoid, and the realistic possibilities which exist at any given time. The significant differences between the pre-war programmes, on the one hand, and the post-war editions of the *BRS* on the other, are a further illustration of the Marxist method of tackling all political issues in the light of prevailing circumstances and on the basis of the experience acquired by the movement, both nationally and internationally. These differences of approach to the forms of the revolution will be examined at greater length in the third chapter of this book.

The final distinctive feature of all Communist Party programmes is that they provide a broad outline of the socialist society which will take the place of capitalism. This is clearly necessary in order to inspire the movement with a vision of its fundamental objectives, but there are a number of dangers involved.

The first one is that the programme might turn into a blueprint and become a list of desirable aims which correspond to the whims and fancies of its authors. In order not to fall into this trap, Marx and Engels carefully omitted any detailed description of socialism before they could draw upon an actual experience. The Paris Commune provided this experience, but its existence was too short (two and a half months) to supply Marx and the movement with anything more elaborate than a few guidelines. After the victory of the 1917 October Revolution in Russia, the situation changed radically: now at last there was a country which had begun to build socialism in a practical way, now at last socialism ceased to be a dream and became a reality for all to see.

However, there immediately appeared a second danger for Communists, that of regarding the Soviet experience as a universal model, requiring only minor modifications before it can be applied to other countries. Soon, a third danger emerged, *viz.* not drawing a distinction between the transitional period which comes immediately after the abolition of capitalism and the period when socialism is firmly established as the basis of society. Lastly, a permanent danger involved in any attempt to describe the future concerns the issues which are not examined, for in this respect, sins of omission can be as serious as those of commission.

How did successive Communist Party programmes manage to steer clear of all these dangers? It must be frankly admitted that none of them has been entirely avoided. With regard to the first one, the worst offenders seem to be the 1968 and 1978 versions of the *BRS*. In their wholly admirable attempt to be as clear as possible about the party's intentions, these two documents at times describe socialist society in Britain as if their authors already knew in advance the precise forms of a future socialist organisation.

It is true that they generally say what a future socialist Britain would do rather than will do, but this is not enough. A political party which is based on the science of Marxism must warn that the predictive powers of any science concern only the general and not the particular, for in the latter case, one must reckon with a host of imponderables. It would have been much better to say that the Communist Party will do everything in its power to ensure that this or that development takes place rather than confidently assert that it would. What is involved here is obviously more than a question of style, but of complete political honesty.

The danger of considering socialism as a universal model, first tested in the Soviet Union, then in Eastern Europe, was not fully avoided until 1958.

The first party programme clearly expected that there would be soviets in Britain just as there were soviets in Russia. The other side of the coin, however, is that in describing the Soviet Britain they were aiming at, the authors of *FSB* showed a remarkable awareness of specific British conditions. *FSB* was not yet a *British Road to Socialism*, but it was a stepping stone towards it.

As for the 1951-52 *BRS*, although it is the first to state emphatically and unequivocally that "Britain will reach socialism by her own road," one cannot say that the subsequent description of this road is altogether happy, for it is presented as involving the transformation "of capitalist democracy into a real People's Democracy". The use of the phrase "People's Democracy" must be assessed in relation to the historical context of the 1950s, when the concept of "models" continued to influence the thinking of all Communists. It was an advance for the international Communist movement and for the CPGB to say that there were now two models, the Soviet one and the East European one, but the point is that the very concept of "models" is wrong for the simple reason that each experience is unique.

The present writer would go further and express his belief that one should not speak of universal laws of socialism because the use of the words "laws" sounds, and is bound to sound, unnecessarily prescriptive. Apart from the general requirements of any form of socialism (common ownership and control of the means of production, planned production for use, and power in the hands of the working class and its allies), the real universality of socialism does not lie in its having a rigid set of laws but rather in the fact that the individual experience of every country shows how outmoded and harmful the profit system is and how historically necessary and logical is the building of a higher form of society based on the principle of "the associated producers rationally regulating their interchange with Nature".[2] Such is dialectical relationship between the general and the particular.

The danger of confusing the transition to socialism period with the socialist period itself is apparent in a mild form in *FSB* and more seriously in the 1951-52 *BRS*, but is successfully overcome in the 1978 *BRS*. To be fair to *FSB*, one should speak not so much of a confusion between two stages but of the programme's exclusive concern with "Soviet power in Britain" as the first step toward building a socialist, then a communist-society.

When Robin Page Arnot introduced *FSB* at the party's 13th congress, he began by saying that it was not the basic party programme "containing all the aims which the party strives to realise", but a "special programme for the immediate situation in the world today". How realistic it was to imagine that Soviet power was on the agenda in 1935 is another matter.

In those days, even the USSR was supposed to be still at the transitional stage, so that the CPGB's reluctance to move further afield in its programme was perhaps understandable. It is for modern readers that such an approach is slightly confusing. On looking at the section "What the British Soviets will do," they will find it difficult to see in what way the various measures which are mentioned are anything but the implementation of socialist policies. Actually, what *FSB* is implying, without actually saying so, is that during the period of soviet power, the capitalist class will have been defeated but not yet abolished.

In the 1951-52 *BRS*, the main tasks of a "People's Government" are mentioned twice, first in relation to the situation which would exist after the British people have elected "a Parliament [which is] truly representative of the people", and secondly in relation to some unspecified stage. It is tempting to suggest that the first occasion refers to the transitional period and the second one to the socialist period, but unfortunately this is far from clear in the text. Apart from the fact that a number of measures which have to be carried out by the People's Government "Mark 1" are the same as those which apply to the People's Government "Mark 2," the latter is expected to "mobilise the overwhelming majority of the people to break the economic and political power of the big exploiters".

Either this is a job which ought to have been the most urgent priority in the transitional period or the programme is not really speaking of different stages. In the latter case, why have two descriptions of the People's Government and often repeat points which have already been made? This is not a "stagist" critique of the 1951-52 *BRS*, for what is at stake is not the drawing of a fixed demarcation line between various stages of a continuous process, but rather the vagueness of the programme with regard to the different problems which have to be faced as the revolution develops.

No such vagueness and confusion can be found in the 1978 *BRS*, as can be seen from its last two chapters which are respectively entitled "Towards socialist revolution" and "Building a socialist Britain." The former includes a section "Next stage in the revolutionary process," in which we can read that:

> The achievement of state power by the working class and its allies will not be a single act, but the culmination of a process of struggle. The length of this process will be determined by the outcome of the struggle at various stages. (p37)

The latter chapter describes the socialist stage and mentions, among other things "the economics of socialism," "socialist democracy," "women and socialism," and so on.

Finally, with regard to omissions, one example should suffice. It concerns the absence from the 1958 *BRS* of any reference to the 20th CPSU congress which ushered in the principled criticism of what is known as "Stalinism," and more generally, the extreme brevity, which almost amounts to an omission, of all the references to the socialist countries and the international Communist movement in all editions of the *BRS*.

No doubt, both the absence and the brevity are due to the very commendable aim of stressing the British character of the CPGB, its complete independence, and its ability to work out its strategy without being unduly influenced by others. Unfortunately, when silence and brevity concern important issues, they can be counter-productive.

The lack of reference to Stalinism in the 1958 *BRS* ignores the well-known fact that a new edition of the CPGB programme became necessary largely as a result of the debates which took place in the international Communist movement after the 20th CPSU congress. British Communists took part in these debates and drew their own conclusions. Why not say so? Why not add that the novel emphasis on socialist democracy is one of the lessons which the CPGB learnt after becoming acquainted with Stalin's bureaucratic distortions?

As for the scanty references to the socialist countries, far from proving the independence of the British party, they give the impression that it is somewhat "embarrassed" by the Soviet Union and other countries where Communists are in power. But we cannot evade the question which is asked by so many non-Communists, from open foes to friendly sympathisers, "What about Russia?". The answer is that "Russia" is an inspiration but not a model, that it is a great force for peace, and that our support is accompanied by constructive criticisms of its limitations. This is another issue to which it will be necessary to return later.

With regard to the international Communist movement, all that the 1978 *BRS* says is that:

> international solidarity is vital not only in the immediate struggles, but for the achievement and building of socialism. (p26)

Is this enough? Surely, another opportunity has been missed to show that independence and solidarity are not mutually exclusive and that the CPGB follows very closely all developments among Communists of other countries, not in order to interfere in their internal affairs or to allow them to interfere in the CPGB's internal affairs, but because of the fact that all CPs share a common ideal, that what any one of them does has repercussions on the rest of the movement, and that from time to time it is imperative to take part in joint struggles against the common enemy. And it is no good claiming that this has nothing to do with a *British Road to Socialism*, for this would be carrying independence to the point of insularity.

NOTES

1 See John Hoffman, *The Gramscian Challenge* (Basil Blackwell, 1984), especially pp.18-50 and pp·76-98.
2 Karl Marx, *Capital*, vol. 3, chapter XLVIII.

2

The Class Approach

As all Communist Party programmes are based on Marxism, we must begin by examining what Marx, Engels and Lenin meant by a class approach. Although the concept of class is central to historical materialism, Marx and Engels did not give an actual definition of it. The last chapter of *Capital*, volume 3, is unfinished and breaks off just as it raises the question "What constitutes a class?".

However, it is possible to infer without much difficulty what the founders of Marxism understood by classes, especially by looking at those texts which specifically deal with their origin and development.[1] It soon becomes clear that the Marxist concept of class is a materialist and a dialectical one. It is materialist inasmuch as the emergence and the evolution of classes are related by Marx to the development of production: classes first arose when higher productivity enabled a minority to live off the labour of the majority, and subsequently, all major changes in the mode of production led to the formation of new classes: "The handmill gives you society with the feudal lord; the steam-mill, society with the industrial capitalist."[2]

Class is also a dialectical concept, first because it is a living relationship rather than a fixed object, and secondly, because the existence of classes means that society is divided into exploiters and exploited and that there is inevitable and irreconcilable conflict of interests between them.

When we come to Lenin, we find that on two occasions he did give a definition of class, but it must be pointed out that his remarks on the subject were incidental to the political issues he was then tackling and thus did not claim to be a fully worked out scientific formulation.

The first occasion was a passage in the 1919 pamphlet, *A Great Beginning*:

Classes are large groups of people which differ from each other by the place they occupy in a historically definite system of social production, by their relation (in most cases fixed and formulated by laws) to the means of production, by their role in the social organisation of labour, and consequently, by the dimensions and method of acquiring the share of social wealth that they obtain. Classes are groups of people one of which may appropriate the labour of another owing to the different places they occupy in the definite system of social economy.[3]

The second occasion was Lenin's speech to the Third Congress of the Russian YCL (1920), in the course of which he declared:

"Classes are that which permits one section of society to appropriate the labour of another section."[4]

The great value of Marxism-Leninism is not that it provides a textbook definition of class, but rather a scientific guideline for finding one's bearings in the world of politics, thus avoiding being taken in by misleading appearances. For, as Lenin wrote:

People always were and always will be the stupid victims of deceit and self-deceit in politics until they learn to discover the interests of some class behind all moral, religious, political and social phrases, declarations and promises.[5]

Now, the ability to discover the essence of reality which lies hidden under layers of superficial appearances is the distinctive characteristic of all science. This is why the class approach of Marxism-Leninism is the only scientific approach to politics, the only one which gets to the heart of the matter. At an international forum of scientists, the Soviet leader Gorbachev pointed to portraits of Marx and Lenin and declared:

These two men taught us that in order to get down to the substance of anything, we should brush the rubbish off the surface and lay bare the motives and interests which underlie one position or another.[6]

To look for any other driving force in politics apart from class interests is to give up the field of ascertainable facts and so to rely on guesswork and impressions. On the other hand, a Marxist party which makes an objective study of the conflicting interests of various classes, both permanent and transient ones, can map out its strategy with the same degree or rigour which can be found among scientists. This, of course, does not mean that

Communists can never make mistakes, for to have a scientific method is one thing, but to know how to apply it correctly in all circumstances is quite another, and here human fallibility and the intrusion of non-scientific prejudices and assumptions play their part.

The fact that all political and social issues are determined by class interests does not mean that human beings are driven by these interests as blindly as animals are driven by instinct. Far from denying that people are motivated by ideas and values, Marxism asserts that it is through ideas and values that men and women become conscious, more or less accurately, of the social conflicts of their time. And this is hardly surprising, since these ideas and values are but the reflections, again, more or less accurate, of class interests. The values of an exploiting class, for example, are always values which tend to justify exploitation, whether the individuals who defend these values are aware of it or not. The values of non-exploiting classes and strata, for their part, are at bottom critical of exploitation.

In order to illustrate the above propositions, let us consider first a well-known Tory value, private enterprise as the embodiment of the freedom of the individual. No deep intuition is needed to realise that the emphasis on the so-called virtues of private or free enterprise merely translates into "decent" language the capitalist's naked interest, which is to make profits without any outside interference. Next, let us look at a value which is much extolled by reformists, the value of "moderation". The class interests represented here are those of a small section of working people who are afraid of losing the few privileges, often illusory and invariably precarious, which the ruling class allows them to enjoy in order to provide itself with allies within the labour movement. Finally, consider the traditional value of militant workers, solidarity. It does not stem from moral principles in the first place, but from the workers' interest in confronting the employers as a united body, for they know from bitter experience that "United we stand, divided we fall."

The scientific interpretation of politics as being governed by class interests does not amount to the cynical view that all political life is dominated by hypocrisy. There is, of course, a good deal of hypocrisy among politicians, or rather among those politicians who uphold a system based on exploitation, because they have a vested interest in falsifying and embellishing the truth. But this does not explain why so many decent people are taken in by politicians or why a small number of these politicians honestly believe in the values they preach. The fact is, as Marx and Engels pointed out, that the ruling ideas of any given time are always the ideas of the ruling class and that such a class is not so much guilty of deception as of self-deception. Its exploiting nature prevents it from seeing the social world as it really is. It has a "false consciousness" of reality, and for so long as its form of exploitation seems to work, this false consciousness spreads to the rest of society. Ideas and values which challenge those of the ruling class emerge only when that ruling class has become a fetter on the further development of production. Today, capitalist ideas have become obsolete because they no longer correspond to the modern level of the productive forces: the social character of production rebels against the private character of ownership and control. The class which is most likely to appreciate this conflict is the class which is vitally interested in abolishing exploitation rather than perpetuating it, the working class. But it does not give up the "false consciousness" of the bourgeoisie automatically. In order to be able to do so, it must be equipped with science. By providing a class approach to politics, all Communist Party programmes have given the British working class the scientific weapon it needs. We shall now examine the main features of this class approach.

It is unfortunate that the phrase "class against class" should belong to a very sectarian period in the CPGB's history because, in its literal sense, it expresses the long-standing Communist view that all modern political conflicts have their roots in the struggle of one class against another class. The party's mistake in 1929 was not to have stressed the class nature of the political struggle, but to have oversimplified it to the point of caricature by tending to dismiss as enemies all those who do not follow the CP's lead. The Communist Party regards the struggle between capitalists and workers as being so crucial that since 1935 all its programmes have devoted their opening pages to it.

FSB, the first party programme, begins with a section which contrasts the wealth and power of the capitalists with the lot of all other sections: poverty and unemployment for the working class, falling incomes and insecurity for the middle strata, the fear of war and the threat of fascism for the British people as a whole. For FSB, the key political question is: "How can the workers end capitalism?" All policies, strategies and tactics must be assessed in relation to this central issue.

The 1939 DP also starts by describing the way in which the capitalist class dominates Britain economically and politically, and then replies to the question "What is to be done?" by asserting that "the answer ... can only be based on a scientific analysis of the existing organisation of society".

The first half of the document is devoted to this scientific analysis.

The same pattern continues to apply to all versions of the BRS. Thus the 1951-52 programme starts with an introduction which refers to the great hopes and possibilities of the immediate post-war period. However, the wealth and power of the capitalist class were not seriously challenged and weakened because of "Labour reformism and Labour imperialism, which is the servant of big capitalist interests". Once again, the solution to Britain's problems is said to depend on the abolition of capitalism.

The introduction of the 1958 BRS also declares that socialism alone "can solve the problems of the British people and end the class divisions of society" and that the people, "led by the working class", must and can build a new society, provided they plan their future on the basis of an understanding of the past and the present. The *BRS* is offered as a contribution to that necessary understanding and necessary planning.

Finally, both the 1968 and the 1978 *BRS* update the case made out by their predecessors and reassert the central role of the class struggle in modern British society. The 1978 version sums up the CPGB's permanent view when it asserts that:

> These monopoly capitalists are the main enemy in the way of democratic, economic and social progress. (p17)

and that:

> The basic force for change in our society is the class struggle between workers and capitalists. (p29)

To many readers, the above reminders of the repeated emphasis on the class struggle in all Communisst Party programmes may appear to be nothing more than the labouring of the obvious. Class politics is indeed "obvious" for a Communist Party, but perhaps it is not sufficiently realised that it is this "obvious" feature which makes it different from other political parties. The latter may, and indeed often do, refer to social divisions, and so indirectly to classes, but their proclaimed ambition is to transcend what they call the "narrow sectional approach" and to speak for the community as a whole. The CP, on the other hand, unashamedly asserts its class nature. It does not hypocritically claim to represent the whole nation, but the great majority of the nation against the small minority which dominates it and exploits it. If a party that calls itself Communist were to lose its class approach, it would simply lose its distinctive class identity. For a Communist party is in business for one reason only – to wage the class struggle.

In order to wage the class struggle successfully (and bring it, paradoxically, to an end), it must always base its policy on an analysis of class forces at a given time. Surprisingly, a detailed class analysis does not appear as such until the 1978 *BRS*. It is only implied in previous programmes, with the possible exception of the 1939 *DP* which devotes one important section of its first chapter to the question of who are "the people" (wage workers, independent producers, farmers and "the free professions," all of whom "are brought more and more into subjection to the monopolist ruling class"). One of the great merits of the 1978 *BRS* is that it fully realises the need for including a class analysis, however brief, because:

> Building the broad democratic alliance involves an under standing of the class forces in capitalist society in Britain. (p17)

The programme then proceeds to discuss the main features of the two main classes, working class and capitalist class, and of the intermediate strata.

Despite its undoubted merits, the section on "classes in capitalist society" in the 1978 *BRS* suffers from two weaknesses. The first one is that it fails to say what Marxists understand by "class". This omission is particularly regrettable in the light of the deliberate attempt by bourgeois writers to deprive the concept of any objective significance. Class, we are told, means different things to different people, which is a subtle way of either ignoring the existence of class divisions or of denying their fundamental importance. Had the *BRS* given a brief definition of "class," by paraphrasing Lenin for example, it would have shown that for Communists classes represent objective realities. Admittedly, the CPGB programme lays great stress on the objective interests of various classes, but it would have been useful to explain that these interests stem from the different position each class occupies in relation to the ownership and control of the means of production rather than from subjective feelings which, in any case, are always hard to ascertain.

The second weakness concerns the definition of the working class, an issue about which there is an ongoing debate among Marxists. Instead of leaving the debate open, the *BRS* somewhat arbitrarily opts for a so-called "broad" definition, viz that the working class includes all those "who sell their labour power, their capacity to work, in return for a wage or salary" (p18). Incidentally, this is the first time that a CPGB programme not only takes the trouble to "define" the working class, but defines it in that way. For example, its immediate predecessor, the 1968 *BRS*, contained no definition, broad or narrow, and furthermore took the view that "teachers and other professional workers" are allies of the working class, not actual members of it, for it declared that their "interests are bound up with those of the working class and the labour movement as a whole". (p26)

According to the present writer, a Marxist definition of the working class must include both the fact that it has to sell its labour power in order to live and that its work produces surplus value.

Naturally the adoption of this definition would also have closed debate. In order not to settle the issue authoritatively in the party programme, the second, third and fourth paragraphs on page 18 could have been rephrased as follows:

> The working class includes both manual and non-manual workers, in other words, all those who are part of what Marx calls "the collective labourer" upon whom capitalism depends for its profits.

> The distinction between manual and mental work is increasingly being broken down by modern processes of production. In particular, technicians, clerical and sales workers are as much members of the working class as engineers, miners, building workers, etc, because they do not own any means of production, depend on the sale of their labour power to capi-

talist employers, and as a rule have no control relationship to the means of production.

The precise "definition" of the working class is a matter of debate among Marxists. Some of them think that the sale of labour power to an employer is a sufficient criterion, whereas others insist that the creation of surplus value is an essential characteristic of the working class under capitalism.

We do not intend to close this debate, but we take the view, which can be shared by all Marxists, that there is a community of interests among all the working people who have to sell their labour power in order to live. For example, those who are engaged in education, in the health service, in the civil service and in local government have objectively the same interests as those who directly contribute to the capitalist production of goods and profits. Though some of these may regard themselves as "middle class," and often work in institutions which help to perpetuate capitalism and its ideas, their interests broadly coincide with those of workers in industry.

The above formulation has the advantage of leaving the debate open at a time when there are genuine Marxists on both sides of the fence. Having said this, however, one must add that like all theoretical debates among Marxists the one concerning the definition of the working class has important practical consequences, and because of this, will have to be settled one way or the other in the near future. In the meantime, it is impossible not to notice that, whatever its validity or otherwise, the "broad" definition has been used by Eurocommunists and revisionists in order to substitute, guardedly at first, the concept of "people" for the concept of "working class". Such a substitution is completely alien to Marxism and is opposed to all the CPGB programmes published so far, including the 1978 *BRS*.

The term "people" certainly figures in the writing of Marxists, but never in lieu of "class". In fact, the "people" includes all the non-exploiting classes and strata in a given nation. Marxists seek both the support and the involvement of the people, ie of more than one class, but they do single out the working class as the one part of the people which can lead all the others in the struggle for socialism. This is not an arbitrary choice but one which stems from the materialist understanding that the working class is the one force which is most directly interested in abolishing capitalist exploitation (and all exploitation at the same time) and which has the ability, the power, the organisation and the experience which are needed for leading the struggle. By singling out the working class as the leading revolutionary force, Marxists do not deny the crucial importance of an alliance between workers and other social classes which suffer under capitalism. In fact, Marx warned long ago that if the working class decided to go it alone, it would have to sing a funeral solo instead of a joyful hymn of victory. Capitalism cannot be defeated by the working class alone, but neither can it be challenged and eventually destroyed unless the working class leads the struggle against it.

This is a point which all Communist Party programmes forcefully make. The one apparent exception seems to be the 1935 *FSB* in that the expression "united struggle," which occurs frequently, applies to working class unity rather than to a broader alliance of non-exploiting classes. It must be remembered that *FSB* was adopted before the CPGB had fully endorsed the Popular Front strategy and that in any case the numerical size of the British working class was bound to put the question of its own unity in the forefront. Moreover, although there is no reference to a popular alliance as such, the role of other classes is not ignored by *FSB*. For example, under the heading "New Democracy" we find the following first paragraph:

> Nor will this true democracy be confined to the industrial workers alone. Those substantial sections of the population, such as technical and professional workers, whose interests are today being sacrificed by the present dictatorial rule of the great capitalists, will play their part in the Workers' Councils. (*FSB*, p26)

We are also informed at the end of the section that the workers' dictatorship:

> ...will not suppress the small men, the petty bourgeoisie, or treat them as though they were big capitalists. On the contrary, the British working class will act towards the small men as their organiser and guide on the path that leads to a classless Socialist society. (*FSB*, p27)

In the 1939 *DP*, the experience of the Popular Front has been assimilated by the CPGB so that it can declare in the section entitled "The immediate programme" that it:

> ...directs all its efforts to rouse and unite the working class, and to rally all progressive and peace-loving sections of the British people for a joint struggle against the monopolist rulers and their reactionary policy. (*DP*, p62)

It is in the successive versions of the *BRS*, however, that the CP's strategy is clarified as resting on a double proposition, viz the leading role of the working class and the need for a broad popular alliance. The two aspects are inseparable from each other, since working-class leadership necessarily implies that there are other forces to be led, and conversely, since an organised alliance requires that a lead be given by its most advanced constituent. In the 1951 *BRS* we read that:

> The working people [amended to "working class" in the 1952 version] of Britain in industry and agriculture form the immense majority of the population and constitute with their families fully two-thirds of the population. To these must be added the great bulk of the clerical and professional workers, the teachers, technicians and scientists, the working farmers, shopkeepers and small businessmen, whose interests are equally threatened by the big land-owning, industrial and financial capitalists, and whose security and future prospects are closely bound up with those of the industrial working class.
>
> Together these represent a mighty political force, fully capable of defeating the present exploiters and rulers of the British people... (1951 *BRS*, p13, 1952 *BRS*, pp10-11)

The 1951-52 *BRS* draws the conclusion that a "broad coalition or popular alliance of all sections of the working people" is needed to open up the path to socialism and that this alliance:

> ...can be built only on the basis of a united working class as its decisive leading force – the class that is most concerned in the struggle for a new order in society. (1951 *BRS*, p15 1952, *BRS*, p13)

The 1958 *BRS* opens with the statement that:

> The Communist Party's aim is socialism, because socialism is the only way to solve the problems of the British people and end the class divisions in society (p5)

and a little further down, expresses its confidence that the working class can lead the struggle for socialism because it:

> ...makes up the great majority of the population. It is also a highly organised working class, with a long tradition of struggle. It has the possibility of winning to its side other sections of the population, people whose interests have nothing in common with those of the handful of monopolists who now dominate our political and economic life. (p9)

Hence the conclusion:

> One thing is clear: socialism can only be built with power in the hands of the people, led by the working class. (ibid)

The 1968 *BRS* describes the Communist Party as a Marxist party, and then adds:

> As Marxists we understand that the interests of the capitalist class and the working class are opposed and cannot be reconciled; that capitalism can and must be ended and replaced; that the working people, led by the working class, must win state power and build a socialist society. (pp18-19)

In the chapter "Next steps ahead," the 1968 *BRS* declares that what is immediately required and possible is:

> ...to build a broad popular alliance around the leadership of the working class... (p28)

This would be an alliance "against monopoly capitalism" (ibid), whose core will be "the working class and its organisations" because it is:

> ...the main class force in the struggle to change society because of its key position in social production. (pp29-30)

Finally, the 1978 version of the *BRS* reasserts that:

> The leading force in the alliance will be the working class, whose interests are most directly opposed to those of the capitalist ruling class, and whose strength and capacity for organisation enables it to give leadership to all the democratic forces in society. (p18)

As for the Communist Party, we are told that:

> ...it must be organised for socialist revolution. It must therefore be firmly rooted in the working class, because of its leading role in society, and especially in the industrial working class. (p26)

What clearly emerges from the way in which all Communist Party programmes have tackled the issue of the leading role of the working class in an anti-capitalist alliance is that such a leading role is not presented as an article of faith, but as being dictated by objective facts. The leading role of the working class is not decreed, it is deduced from reality. It is true that this reality is always changing – a fact which Marxism stresses – and that, consequently, the nature and composition of the working class are never quite the same from one period to another, but so long as we live under capitalism, the fact remains that the only class which is best equipped to challenge the system is the working class. As Marx and Engels put it long ago in the 1848 Manifesto: "what the bourgeoisie produces above all is its own grave-diggers".

This truth is so embedded into the thinking of a Communist Party that in order to attack it, revisionists have to use devious means. It is rare to find leading revisionists openly rejecting the leading role of the working class, for their credibility demands that they should continue to pay lip service to it. At the same time, they talk so much about changes, real or imaginary, about weaknesses, again real or imaginary, and about the emergence of dynamic "new social forces," that the overall effect of their statements and allegedly learned analyses is to undermine people's confidence in the ability of the working class to be an effective agent of social change.

If the revisionist attempt is successful, it will compel the CPGB to repudiate the most important feature of all its previous programmes. Such a radical transformation would be a disaster, not because Communists are afraid of changing with the times when a changing reality demands it, but on the contrary, because the revisionist project runs counter to reality. It is not in the name of dogmatism and orthodoxy that Marxist-Leninists utterly reject it, but in the name of realism. Let us therefore briefly examine what amounts to the revisionist case against the Communist Party's reasoned belief in the leading role of the working class.

The two most frequent revisionist arguments are, first, that the working class has changed dramatically in the last few years, and secondly, that new "forces" or "movements" – notice, not classes – are doing a better job against "the Establishment" than the traditional proletariat. The full treatment of the first issue is outside the scope of the present study, and readers are strongly advised to consult the writings of Marxist economists and sociologists, the most important of which are mentioned in the note at the end of this chapter.[7]

Here, we can only focus on some of the salient aspects, but before examining them one should bear in mind that just as the British working class has altered in the last 20 years or so, so it will continue to change both in the immediate and in the more distant future. While it is impossible to foresee future changes in every detail, Marxists are more concerned with general trends, or to use Marx's own terminology, with the way in which "the general law of motion" of capitalism manifests itself, not so much in spite of the changes which constantly occur, but rather through these very changes. The essence of capitalism is the pursuit of profit, whose one and only source is the surplus value produced by the labour of the working class. When Marxists study the way in which the working class of any one country evolves, they do not confine themselves to mere description and statistics, but they try to find the answer to the following question: in what way does this or that change affect the basic role of the working class as a class whose labour produces surplus value? Let us for one minute enter the realm of science fiction and imagine that capitalism has at last discovered a way of making profits without relying on workers' labour. Then and then only, will it be possible to ask whether the working class has ceased to be a revolutionary force. But then, in such a fantastic case, revolution itself will have become unnecessary.

Among the most striking changes which have affected the British working class in recent years, two which stand out (and are related) are its numerical decline and its new composition. There is no doubt that there has been a decline in the number of those workers "in the basic extractive, transport and manufacturing industries," as the 1978 *BRS* points out, adding incidentally that this section continues "to play a leading role in the working class movement" (p19). But the revolutionary role of the working class does not depend on its numerical size, although in a country such as Britain this has been an important factor in determining the forms of its struggle; it depends, as has been frequently emphasised throughout these pages, on its position in the production process. Moreover, if workers in the traditional industries such as coal, steel and textiles have decreased in numbers, there has been, on the other hand, a new influx into the working class with the number of people engaged in such industries as electronics, aeronautics and so on.

There has also been an increase in the number of white-collar workers and the growth of a "service industry". These changes, we are confidently told, have downgraded the role of the traditional "proletariat". Before going any further, let us be quite clear that for Marxists, the proletariat has never been confined to manual workers. It was none other than Marx him self who showed in *Capital* that the working class should be regarded as a "collective labourer," ie that the various divisions of labour which exist within its ranks mean that all sections, rather than a single privileged one (the industrial workers), contribute to the production of surplus value.

Today, under the impact of the scientific and technological revolution, the working class as a "collective labourer" is increasingly made up of both manual and mental workers. In many branches of industry, manual labour involves a considerable amount of mental labour, and vice-versa. Moreover, white-collar workers no longer enjoy special "perks" or higher wages. As a result they have, of their own accord, adopted the "traditional" methods of struggle of the labour movement: militant unionism, strikes and so on. As for the so-called "service economy," its importance in modern Britain should not be exaggerated. According to Ron Bellamy, only 36% of the total workforce can be found in the service sector. The same writer also shows that "different sectors, including those usually classified as services, are being brought together into an organic whole", with the result that they are all part of the "collective labourer" already mentioned.

Some of the specific features of the British economy in the present period are that it has become a low-wage, low-productivity and low-investment economy. The first two aspects are a direct consequence of the domination of the multinational corporations, while the last one is also due to the fact that British capitalists have tended to invest their capital overseas rather than at home or in finance and speculation rather than in industry. In addition, the level of unemployment around the 4 million mark (among the highest in the western world) is no transient phenomenon but it belongs, as it were, to the fittings and fixtures of British capitalism in decay. That all these developments have weakened the working class cannot be denied. Nor should one underestimate the harmful effects of anti-union legislation, of which the first steps were taken by a Labour government and which has since been "perfected" by the Tories.

However, to speak of a long-term and/or irreversible decline of the labour movement is defeatist and inaccurate. It is defeatist because in over-stressing the strength of the enemy it ignores its basic weakness: yes, capitalism is doing its utmost to weaken the working class, economically, politically and ideologically, but none of its desperate and vicious measures can alter the fact that it has had its day. It can no longer deliver the goods.

Talk of an irreversible decline is also inaccurate for two reasons. One is that a great many of the changes which have affected the working class are due to political decisions by the ruling class, and so can be challenged and reversed by mass struggle. The second reason is that such a challenge has in fact already started. How can one talk about a demoralised working class and forget the year-long miners' strike? How can one describe British workers as spineless and take no notice of British workers' resistance to Rupert Murdoch? And if revisionists and reformists join forces to proclaim that the miners "lost" and to announce that the printworkers could not win, we must remind them of their own responsibility and shameful role. If there had been fewer articles suggesting a "halt" in "the forward march of Labour" and more practical work in key industries (such as undertaken by the CPGB in 1972-71), the situation would not be as bad as it is today. Without in the least denying that the battle against the Tories and their system has become harder, that it is bound to have its full share of defeats as well as victories, the duty of genuine communists or socialists is to keep the spirit of resistance alive.

Not for sentimental nor nostalgic reasons, but because long experience has shown repeatedly that such resistance is a historical necessity it is true that capitalism, and British capitalism in particular, has shown that it has not yet exhausted its ability to survive, but every new lease of life it has managed to give itself has been unable to end its economic crises and to do away with its political and moral bankruptcy. Sooner or later, such a sys tem will have to go. But the sooner the better, and this depends on what we do now. In other words, the leading role of the working class becomes a most urgent practical issue.

Not content with casting doubts about the ability of the working class to lead the struggle for socialism, the revisionists devote most of their attention to the new "movements" and the new "forces" which have emerged since the Sixties and which they effectively present as alternatives to the labour movement. On this issue, the 1978 BRS suffers from a minor weakness – which is fully exploited by the revisionists, but it also contains a major strength – which the revisionists endeavour to forget. Let us deal with the weakness first. It consists in the loose way in which terms such as "movements" and "forces" are used and described:

> So movements and groupings develop which may not belong to a major class (for example, students) or embrace people from different classes and strata (for example, black, national, women's, youth, environmental, peace and solidarity movements). Hence the broad democratic alliance needs to be not an expression of class forces, but of other important forces in society which emerge out of areas of oppression not always directly connected with the relations of production. (p29)

The above formulation is confusing in that it gives the impression that there are two kinds of "forces" in society – class forces and other forces. But this is a very undialectical view because it assumes an artificial division of social issues into "class" and "non-class" whilst ignoring the interconnections which link all the problems which confront modern society. With regard to students, we are told that they do "not belong to a major class". What does this mean? Do they belong to a minor class?

As for the other "movements," it is not terribly helpful to state the obvious by saying that they "embrace people from different classes", without adding that there is one class at least which does not and cannot take part in these anti-establishment movements, namely, the one class which constitutes the establishment, the monopoly capitalist class. Individual members of this class who join any of these movements are the exception rather than the rule, and above all, they do not commit the whole of their class.

Another misleading statement is the reference to "areas of oppression not always directly connected with the relations of production". As it stands, this statement is bound to bring grist to the mill of those who declare that classes are exclusively economic entities and that the class struggle, being "directly connected with the relations of production", is exclusively an economic struggle. Again, such an approach is undialectical – and unhistorical

to boot. Classes came into being on an economic basis, but once constituted they inevitably created their own political institutions and their own ideology as well as generated additional forms of oppression. Racism is a case in point. Of course, it is not directly connected with the relations of production, but are not its roots to be found in the imperialist exploitation of so-called "inferior" races? And above all, can it be eradicated without a bitter fight against the ideas and practice of a given class, a class which occupies a privileged position in respect of the relations of production and is the main obstacle (though not the only one) standing in the way of racial equality?

A better formulation than the one to be found in the 1978 *BRS* would be something along the lines: capitalism not only exploits people at work, it impinges on every aspect of their lives. This is why the struggle against the system takes many forms and involves a number of movements which have arisen independently to challenge this or that injustice or inequality. In the broad democratic alliance there is room for all these movements, irrespective of the fact that their participants and founders do not think in class terms in the first place, because the broad democratic alliance is simply another phrase for the fact that the working class and other non-exploiting classes and strata fight together on a multitude of issues, some economic, some social, some political, some ideological and some moral.

A brief digression is necessary here in order to clarify what is meant by building a broad democratic alliance. Some Communists genuinely believe that it means founding a broad organisation which people join as individuals or as members of a political party or as participants in a "movement." Such an attitude can best be described as "frontist" in the sense that it corresponds to a now obsolete Communist tactic of setting up a front with limited and transient aims, eg the Popular Front against fascism in the 1930s. But the broad democratic alliance of today should mean something quite different. It is not a federation which people may or may not join, for the simple reason that what is aimed at is not a formal organisation with its own structure and constitution, but a relationship between the organised working class and all those who challenge the ruling class.

In a sense, we might say that the broad democratic alliance will never exist, in the manner in which a political party or a "movement" exists, because it will always be in the making. Moreover, building the broad democratic alliance does not mean signing formal agreements with this or that movement, although, of course, such agreements are not precluded. Building the alliance means two things, which are complementary. First, it means that the labour movement, and especially its Communist component, must itself take up all the issues which arise out of capitalist rule, directly or indirectly, the issues of peace, women's liberation, ethnic minorities' rights, young people's rights, the environment, and so on. Secondly, it means that in the course of its own campaigns on these issues, the labour movement will give support to existing movements outside its ranks, work within them, and provide constructive criticism when needed (eg. criticise the views that all men or all whites are the enemy).

If we now turn to the chief strength of the 1978 *BRS*, we shall find that it brings out forcefully both the need for uniting and co-ordinating the various social movements and the fact that in essence they all share an anticapitalist character. The aim, according to the *BRS*, is not simply to "challenge the position of the ruling class on a series of different issues," but rather "its overall domination" (p33). As for the labour movement, if it must take up the fight on this wide variety of issues, it is not because it ought to pay attention to allegedly non-class issues, but rather – and this time the *BRS* is quite unambiguous – because:

> ...*class oppression* and the struggle against it extend far beyond the workplace and embrace strata beyond the working class. (ibid, my emphasis – MA)

Moreover, the *BRS* urges the working class to "win over to its side other strata which are also the victims of monopoly"(p34). For Eurocommunists, the broad democratic alliance is an alliance for democracy, but it does not seem to be directed against anyone. For the *BRS*, the fight for democracy is in itself a fight against monopoly.

On the issue of democracy, the contrast between Eurocommunists and the *BRS* is at its sharpest. In its usual undialectical way, Eurocommunism draws a mechanistic distinction between "democratic issues" and "class issues" and has the nerve to accuse its opponents of this very crime!

According to Dave Cook, the anti-revisionists "reinterpret the concept of the broad democratic alliance to downgrade the importance of issues of democracy and oppression",[9] falsely posing these against class issues. But this is the very opposite of the truth: the anti-revisionists argue that democratic issues are class issues, and it is not they who falsely pose democracy against class.

To recognise the class nature of democratic issues is not to "downgrade" them, but on the contrary, to afford them their true stature, their revolutionary character. And this is in line with the *BRS*. To begin with, the party programme states that:

> Wide and diverse sections of the people have been reacting against the adverse effect of capitalism and capitalist policies on their lives. (p17)

This means that all those who react against the lack of democracy in modern Britain are objectively reacting against "capitalism and capitalist policies". Moreover, when the *BRS* talks of building a broad democratic alliance, it does not assume that the basis for such an alliance will be found in the realm of ideology, in the love of democracy which characterises the British people, for example. The 1978 *BRS* considers that:

> The objective basis for this [the alliance] is that those who own and control the monopolies which dominate the economic and political system in Britain are only a tiny minority of the people. (ibid)

Finally, the *BRS* does not regard the struggle for democracy as radically different from the struggle for socialism. It does not say: First, let us have democracy, then we shall see about socialism. What it does say is rather: Let us fight for democracy because this is part of the many-sided process which leads to socialism. The following is how it views the tasks of the labour movement:

> The labour movement therefore needs to end the policy of "managing capitalism" and instead to take a course which challenges capitalist power, and, by helping to build the broad democratic alliance, opens the way to change in the direction of socialism. (p35)

It is worth noticing that it is because it has a class approach to the issue of democracy that the *BRS* can reject the formalist view that democracy exists only through its institutions and that extra-parliamentary struggle is undemocratic. On the contrary, says the *BRS*, it is the reformist strategy, "based entirely on the ballot box", which represents a severe curtailment of democracy, because:

> The mass of the people are accorded a strictly limited voting role, and MPs are regarded as little more than lobby fodder. (ibid)

Mass struggle outside Parliament is essential, not only because it is a "political educator" as well as a "weapon for breaking the resistance of the monopolists", but also because it involves the democratic control by the people of their representatives.

The discussion of democracy in terms of its class basis is not confined to the 1978 version of the *BRS*, but can be found in all the programmes which came before it. In the 1929 manifesto we are told that capitalist rule:

> ...is maintained by an apparatus of class dictatorship in the interests of property. (p10)

and that:

> There can be no real democracy unless it is a workers' democracy that is in power. Real democracy means the mass of the population being at once voters and administrators. (p32)

Simply to dismiss these statements because they belong to our sectarian past and because they led to the view that the only kind of democracy was the participatory democracy of workers' councils (ie soviets) is to throw out the baby with the bath water.

It was true in 1929 and it is still true today that even in the most advanced capitalist countries, capitalist rule is incompatible with real democracy, and the point made by the 1935 *FSB* is as valid as ever:

> So long as the employer is the dictator in the factory, so long as the landlord is the dictator in the street, so long as the capitalist class everywhere holds the positions of real power in its hands, there can be no real democracy. (p26)

What is missing from the 1929 manifesto, and to a lesser extent from *FSB*, is the recognition that in a country such as Britain, democratic rights do exist, even under capitalism. Such recognition would not have amounted to a grudging concession, first, because these rights had to be fought for, and secondly, because the struggle to maintain them and extend them is part of the working-class struggle for socialism.

In this respect, the 1939 *DP* represents an advance. The chapter on "Democracy and the State in Britain" opens with the statement that:

> By tenacious struggle and sacrifice the workers in Britain have won right after right from the ruling class ... The existing democratic rights are the heritage of generations of struggle. (p17)

The *DP* warns, however, that "although the people are nominally sovereign, the capitalist class rules" (ibid) and that the peoples in the colonies do not enjoy any such rights, It rightly draws attention to "the limits of capitalist democracy" (p20), and while making the then extremely topical point that it is preferable to fascism, it shows itself aware of the difference in nature between democracy under an exploiting system and democracy under socialism.

Without explicitly saying so, it implies something which had never been in doubt among Marxists until Eurocommunists started to challenge it, namely, that socialist democracy is not a mere extension of capitalist democracy, but its revolutionary transformation. In fact, in order to extend the rights won under capitalism so that they include the basic rights to work, to housing, health, education and leisure, what is needed is a revolution.

The point is made forcefully in the 1951-52 *BRS*, first when it denounces the fashionable (even then!) theory of "democratic socialism" peddled by the reformist leaders of the LP as a "screen behind which they seek to justify their defence of the system of capitalist profit and exploitation" (p10), and secondly when it points out that:

> Despite the democratic rights which have so far been won by the struggles of the people, the real power in Britain is still concentrated in the hands of the tiny section of the rich property-owners (p11)

and draws the revolutionary conclusion that:

> The people cannot advance to socialism, therefore, without real political power ... Only by this means can democracy become a reality. (p12)

(Note: Page references are to the 1952 edition, whose text on the above points is exactly the same as the 1951 *BRS*.)

In the 1958 *BRS*, there is an entirely new section on "Socialist democracy", which is obviously the result of the deep thinking that went on throughout the CPGB after the attack on Stalinist bureaucracy at the 20th CPSU congress.

The temptation was therefore great to adopt a bourgeois liberal standpoint by transcending the allegedly "narrow" class approach, and it must be admitted that voices were then heard in the international Communist movement which yielded to just that kind of temptation. There is no sign of it in the 1958 *BRS*. The CPGB programme repeats the point that:

> In spite of the great advances won by the people in their struggle for a better life, real power in Britain is still in the hands of the small group of very rich families who own more than half the wealth of the country and draw immense sums from the exploitation of colonial peoples. (p22)

In view of this, the *BRS* declares that the economic measures it had outlined earlier need:

> to go hand in hand with more directly political measures to end the supremacy of the rich, build up a socialist state, and establish working class control, that is, socialist democracy, in every aspect of social life. (p23)

The qualitative difference between capitalist democracy and socialist democracy is emphasised, especially in statements like the following:

> Our present form of democracy is largely passive. A Socialist government will develop a much more active democracy in which the ordinary citizen directly controls and administers affairs. (ibid)

The temptation to treat democracy in a bourgeois liberal fashion must have been very great once more in the aftermath of the Czechoslovak crisis of 1968, especially since people both outside and inside the Communist movement loudly proclaimed the opposition between the "socialism with a human face" of the Czechoslovak Action Programme, reputedly "democratic", and the socialism existing in the Soviet Union, reputedly "bureaucratic".

Although the CPGB was clearly split on these issues, and although those who were particularly vocal were either open revisionists or entrenched dogmatists, the 1968 *BRS* avoided both extremes. On the one hand, it stated that:

> It must be the main concern of the labour and popular movement to use and defend every democratic right won in the past, whilst working for a general extension of democratic liberties. (p39)

But, on the other hand, it continued to stress the class nature of the democratic struggle by saying that:

> Every step extends the people's control over the affairs of the country weakens the power of big business. (ibid)

The same balance was maintained in the section on "Socialist democracy," with the introduction of such novelties as pluralism, for example, and yet the reminder that:

> A socialist government requires a socialist state machine.(p53)

The 1968 *BRS* also spoke of the "extension" of democracy, but in the crucial field of industrial democracy, it made it quite clear that such an "extension" cannot occur until and unless there has been a socialist revolution:

> The great extension of industrial democracy, with workers having the dominant say in determining environment and conditions of work, becomes possible with the removal of barriers between workers and management. *This comes about with the elimination of the irreconcilable conflict between them, which exists as long as private ownership is the basis of production.* (p54 – my emphasis, MA)

The only point which now requires brief discussion is whether in adopting a class approach Marxist-Leninists are guilty of "class reductionism". According to Eurocommunists, there is no doubt that this is the case: anti-revisionists say that all issues are class issues, so they "reduce" everything to class!

The formulation "All social issues are class issues" is substantially correct, but it can be misleading if it is not clarified as meaning that all social issues have a class basis. If this is what is meant by the "crime" of "class reductionism", then Marxist-Leninists must indeed plead guilty. Actually, however, the phrase "class reductionism", which was coined by the revisionists, is quite meaningless and is even a contradiction in terms, for it amounts to confusing any phenomenon with its basis, which is ridiculous. If any given issue were entirely contained in its basis, the latter would not be a basis at all but the issue itself.

When Marxists say that all social issues have a class basis, they do not deny that each one has its own characteristics and even that these can react on the basis itself, they are merely applying the elementary – but crucial principle of historical materialism that in a class society all social developments are linked to the class struggle. In some cases, the link is immediately apparent, on wages for example; in many other cases, it is not so apparent, and most of those involved do not see it, but it is the task of science to bring it to light.

According to Martin Jacques, one should recognise:

> ...the centrality of the class contradiction, but alongside that the existence and autonomy of other forms of contradiction (eg. race, sex, nationality, etc.)[10]

This is a most un-Marxist way of presenting the matter. For Marxism, one must recognise the primacy of class, and on that basis (not "alongside" it!) the existence of a host of issues.

Let us, for example, consider the broadest of all existing "movements," the peace movement. Marxist-Leninists assert that this movement came into being as a response to the policies of the capitalist class, in Britain, and in other imperialist countries, which are based on the arms race as a means of "containing" or "rolling back" communism, socialism, democracy, national liberation, in fact anything that threatens the profit system.

This does not mean that all those who want peace are aware of the link between their aspirations and class realities. Many of them are not, and in this respect the peace movement is. not different from other movements in which those who take part are not motivated by a class understanding. This does not dismay Marxists in the least, for they are accustomed to the distinction which must always be drawn between subjective feelings and objective reality. They do not ascribe a class character to an issue in the light of what people think or feel about it, but in the light of its objective significance, whether such significance is perceived by the participants or not.

Moreover, the class character of the peace issue (and of other social issues) means that its solution ultimately depends on the defeat of one class, the capitalist class, and on the victory of another, the working class.

It is in the nature of capitalism to drive to war (as the history of our century shows only too well), and peace will never be secure until socialism has taken over.

Since 1960, the international Communist movement has expressed its confidence that war can be banished from the face of the earth, even before the world victory of socialism, but on one condition – the constant vigilance of the people, and of the working class in the first place. The document adopted by 81 Communist parties in 1960 stated that the possibility of excluding world war from the life of society has arisen, not because the imperialists have been belatedly "converted" to peace and to peaceful coexistence with socialism, but because the balance of class forces has definitely changed to their disadvantage: they are now challenged by a strong socialist camp, a strong national-liberation camp, and a more militant working class at home.

Finally, the stress on the class basis of all social issues does not involve Communists in any kind of sectarianism, for it would be contrary to Marxism to expect or demand ideological clarity from non-Marxists before action, before practice.

As historical materialists, Communists know that correct ideas are always the result of activity and experience, and this is why they do not exist as a pre-condition for joint action that non-Communists should share their understanding of capitalist society. To stick to the example of peace, they are prepared to work with all those who want to save mankind from a nuclear holocaust whether they think that war is caused by lack of faith in God, by human nature, or by any other factor. However, while always putting action first, they hope to bring others to their viewpoint with the help of patient argument.

But perhaps all this is an academic? What does it matter, an impatient reader might exclaim, whether you say that peace is a class issue and the revisionists say that it isn't, as long as you both work for peace? The answer is that this not an academic debate, but a very practical one for Communists.

For example, it is because Marxist-Leninists understand the class basis of the peace issue that they reject the dangerous theory that the two "superpowers", the USA and the USSR, are equally to blame for the arms race. Sadly, such a view has been echoed by people who call themselves Communists! But the fact is that the USA and the USSR are not just two "superpowers", for they have an entirely different class character. One is an imperialist power the other is a socialist power. The threat of thermonuclear war comes from imperialism, not from socialism, and it is the special responsibility of

Communists to hammer this point home. They cannot and do not expect all the peace campaigners to endorse their assessment, but they can and do expect them to be won over by facts. Of these, one of the most important is that peace initiatives usually come from the Soviet Union, not from the United States.

The class approach of Communists enables them to be in the forefront of the struggle against anti-Sovietism, that most dangerous enemy of the peace movement. The so-called "Russian threat" is the one argument used western imperialists to justify the arms race. Communists are particularly well placed to give short shrift to this spurious argument. Inside the broad peace movement, this is their historic distinctive responsibility.

NOTES

1   The writings of Marx which are particularly relevant are:
(a) The letter to Joseph Wedemeyer, in which he relates the existence of classes to "historical phases in the development of production" (5 March 1852), and
(b) *The Preface to the Critique of Political Economy* 1859, in which he asserts that social relations correspond to definite stages of the development of the material forces of production.
In the case of Engels, the relevant writings are:
(a) *The Origin of the Family*, in which he describes the emergence of classes after the dissolution of the primitive commune, and
(b) *Anti-Duhring* and *Ludwig Feuerbach*, in which he describes the formation of the bourgeoisie and the proletariat in modem times.
To the above, one must of course add the famous *Manifesto of the Communist Party*.
2   Karl Marx, *The Poverty of Philosophy* (Chapter 2, "Second Observation").
3   Lenin, *Selected Works*, vol. 9, pp432-33.
4   Ibid. p476.
5   Lenin, "The Three Sources and Three Component Parts of Marxism", in *Selected Works*, vol. 11, pp7-8.
6   *Soviet News*, 16 July 1986, p322.
7   The following are especially recommended:
(a) Ron Bellamy's articles in *World Marxist Review* (July 1984, pp73-79) and in the *Morning Star* (14 and 15 November 1984).
(b) Vadim Zagladin's *Pravda* article, reproduced in the *Morning Star* (4 April 1986).
(c) *Class Politics – An Answer to its Critics* by Ben Fine, Laurence Harris, Marjorie Mayo, Angela Weir and Elizabeth Wilson (Leftover pamphlets, 1984).
(d) Ellen Mieksins Wood's book, *The Retreat from Class- A New "True" Socialism* (Verso, 1986). May I also draw attention to my own article on the role of the working class today in the first issue of *Communist Campaign Review* (September 1986).
8   Ron Bellamy in the *Morning Star*, 14 November 1984.
9   Dave Cook, "No Private Drama," in *Marxism Today* (February 1985)
10 Martin Jacques, EC Report, (*Morning Star*, 22 November 1984).

3

Socialism

The building of a socialist Britain (called Soviet Britain in 1935) has been the aim of all Communist Party programmes. In order to map out a *British Road to Socialism*, they all had to deal with the three aspects involved in the concept of socialism, viz a critique of the existing system, capitalism; an analysis of the way in which capitalism can be ended, the socialist revolution; and an outline of the socialist society which the working class and its allies intend to build in this country. Let us briefly examine the CPGB's evolution on these three issues, as reflected in its programmes.

(a) Critique of capitalism

The socialist case against capitalism is economic, social, political, ideological and moral. Economically, capitalism stands indicted because it rests on exploitation and is incapable of overcoming its basic contradiction, the contradiction between the social character of production and the private character of ownership and control.

The word "exploitation" is not an emotive term for Marxists. It simply describes the fact that ever since the division of society into classes, a minority has been able to live off, ie to exploit, the labour of the majority.

That point is lucidly made in the 1939 *DP*, which devotes a whole chapter to popularising the Marxist analysis of capitalism, and more briefly in the *BRS*.

As for the crisis of British capitalism, we have already seen that each successive programme analysed it in the light of the circumstances existing at the time. A comparison between the various documents brings out very sharply the accuracy of the Communist Party's forecasts that the capitalist crisis would be getting increasingly worse.

For example, whereas the 1958 *BRS* warned that "even when there is relative prosperity... in the background is the threat of widespread economic crisis" (p7), such a crisis was no longer a mere "threat" in 1978, it could be described as an existing fact, fully justifying the opening remark that:

> In Britain the first capitalist power, once the most powerful of all, the crisis is especially deep. (p13)

A little further down, facts and figures are given to show the "disastrous" effects of "the contradictions of the British economy and the policies of successive governments" (ibid).

The social consequences of the capitalist crisis, ie the ways in which its effects have to be borne by the people, are mentioned in all the programmes, again in the light of the situation prevailing at the time.

What capitalism meant to the British people in the 1930s is vividly described in the 1935 *FSB* and in the 1939 *DP*. The former document points out that:

> Poverty, insecurity and malnutrition making their inroads in the homes of millions of workers ... The masses of the people of Britain are being ruined by the big trusts and their millionaires. (pp16-17)

The picture presented by the *DP* is no less grim:

> ...continuous waste of human lives and material resources... Whole areas, once great centres of production, have been allowed to become derelict... For the past two decades over 1 million workers ... have been unemployed; The proportion of parasitic services and luxury occupations grows at the expense of productive industry. Only a little over half the employed workers are today engaged in productive industry... The vital forces of the nation are drained by recurring economic crises. (pp8-9)

After the war, the people were determined that there would be no return to these appalling conditions, and by massively voting for a Labour government, they were able to impose a number of significant improvements, including a progressive health and social security service. But in 1951-52, the *BRS* could sadly remark that:

> No basic social change took place under its [the Labour gov-

ernment's] rule.

And its 1958 successor pointed out that:

> Social services are being cut instead of expanded. Instead of
> confidence in the future, there is a growing feeling of insecu-
> rity. (p5)

However, the same document conceded that "many advances (had) been
won", but it rightly complained that:

> ...the social services in the so-called welfare state are far below
> the level that is possible today. (p7)

By 1968, the position had become so much worse that one could no longer
speak of the "welfare state" and its limitations, for that was a thing of the
past. Instead, the *BRS* of that year devoted a long section to "The People and
the Crisis," in which the attack on the social consequences of capitalism was
particularly strong.

A superficial glance at successive CPGB programmes might give the impression that their indictment of capitalism became sharper over the years.
In a sense, this is true, but only because of the steady worsening of the crisis
and its effects! This time, it was no longer a question of saying how much
more could have been done, but of showing how little had been achieved,
with the result that:

> ...in a period when technical advance has leapt ahead, there
> has been a steady growth of poverty. (p15)

Instead of fulfilling the high hopes of the immediate post-war period, governments after governments have done little but destroy them. For example:

> The funds for social services have been grossly inadequate –
> lower, as a proportion of the Gross National Product than most
> countries of Western Europe. (ibid)

As for the contrast between the development of private enterprise estates
and the number of slums and homeless families, the *BRS* remarked that:

> There is no more vivid example of private affluence leading to
> private squalor. (pp15-16)

Finally, the 1978 *BRS* revealed the following facts about Britain, which was
once described as the richest country in the world:

According to the Royal Commission on the Distribution of Income and Wealth, reporting in 1975, the richest 5% of the population owned nearly half the total wealth. The bottom 80% owned less than a fifth... Some 13 million people live on or near the official poverty line. They include those on low wages, old people, unemployed, one-parent families, and many who are sick or disabled. (p8)

Gone were the modest advances in living standards which were made in the 1950s. Instead:

The modest rise in living standards was slowed down, then halted, and finally turned into a fall. (p13)

One of the worst social consequences of capitalism is the growth of racism, about which the 1978 *BRS* had this to say:

Fascist and racist organisations have taken advantage of the worsening situation in Britain to put the blame for social and economic problems on the 2.5% of the population who are black. Full advantage is being taken of the deep-rooted racist ideas which have resulted from Britain's colonialist history. (p14)

The way in which the CPGB tackled the political case against capitalism, viz that it is incompatible with real democracy, has already been examined in the previous chapter, but in a general way. We should now look at the most important specific points made in successive programmes. In *FSB*, the attack is directed against the form taken by capitalist rule in Britain, the parliamentary system. Although the authors of *FSB* draw the erroneous conclusion that a socialist Britain would have no use at all for Parliament (a point which is further discussed later on in this chapter), their assessment of the capitalist state machine (which includes Parliament) is far from inaccurate. First, *FSB* is right when it says that Parliament only "registers formal decisions" (isn't this a case for its transformation rather than its abolition?) and that effective rule is exercised by the Cabinet, the civil service, the police, the armed forces and the judges. Secondly, it is difficult for today's revolutionaries not to associate themselves with such questions as:

How can this whole machinery, officered by the boss class, be expected faithfully to serve the interests of the working class? How can policemen, drilled in bludgeoning the workers, and kowtowing to the gentry, be expected to act as protectors of the workers' common property? And the highly paid upper class judges? As well ask-how can the leopard change its spots? (p24)

Would not today's miners and printworkers feel inclined to ask the same questions? In reading what their predecessors wrote about the much vaunted capitalist democracy, modern Communists are bound to share their indignation and to admire their revolutionary insight, even if they have to criticise the limitations and weaknesses of their analysis.

The analysis presented in the 1939 *DP* is more subtle, and consequently, the practical conclusions which are advocated tend to be less rigid. As already pointed out, the imperative need in the 1930s to defend bourgeois democracy against fascism led Communist parties, including the CPGB, to attach considerably more importance to the democratic gains already made. However, an additional criticism of capitalism in the political field was precisely that it contained within itself the seeds of fascism. Thus, the *DP* warned that:

> In some countries the capitalist class has abolished the democratic forms and established open terrorist dictatorship or fascism. Strong tendencies in this direction exist also in Britain ... Only the overthrow of capitalist rule ... will lay the basis for full democracy for the people. (pp20-21)

The *DP* also noted that:

> In Britain, the most reactionary sections of the ruling class openly support fascism and collaborate closely with the foreign fascist powers. (p31)

An interesting aspect of the *DP*'s subtler analysis of political life in Britain is the paragraph devoted to "The Feudal Survivals in the Constitution," such as the hereditary monarchy, the House of Lords, and so on, which the capitalist class maintained after "having won power by violent revolution and civil war", because it was "afraid of the further advance of the people, whose armies had won the revolution". Thus, the present British state is an:

> ...alliance of all the sections of the exploiters against the people of the landowners, merchants, financiers and the later industrial capitalists, under cover of a puppet monarchy and aristocratic trappings... (p18)

The 1951-52 *BRS* gives examples of the undemocratic character of the electoral system, such as the parliamentary majority secured by the Tories in 1951 with only 48% of the poll, and points to the fact that:

> The traditional two-party system in Britain has assured effec-
> tive capitalist control, and the frustration of the will of the peo-
> ple... The right-wing leaders of the Labour Party have adapted
> themselves to the policy and interests of the capitalists... (p11)

The document also draws attention to the capitalist control of the civil service, the armed forces, the judiciary, the diplomatic and colonial services,
and the media, and in the light of the facts, it concludes that:

> Democracy under present conditions is restricted for the ma-
> jority of the people by the privilege and power of the wealthy
> few and their agents... (ibid)

The 1958 *BRS* does not repeat or update this analysis, but contents itself
with the remark that:

> The political power of the rich is founded on their economic
> power. (p9)

However, the 1968 and 1978 programmes give more details about the forms
taken by the political power of the rich. In the former, there is a long section
in the first chapter, entitled "Political Power," which shows that, although
governments come and go, "the key officials of state go on", that "Parliament is bypassed more and more as the power of the executive grows", that
trade union democracy is under attack", and that "the growth of monopoly
is now incompatible with democracy" (p10). As for the 1978 *BRS*, it declares
that:

> Government is divorced from the people. Bureaucratic control
> by the state has increased as local democracy has been eroded.
> The ruling class tries to confine democracy to the right to vote
> in elections, and deny the people real participation in decision-
> making. (p6)

The condemnation of capitalism on ideological and moral grounds can be
found in the majority of CPGB programmes when they describe the superiority of socialism over capitalism. Thus, in *FSB*, it is in the third section,
"What the British Soviets will do" that we are told of the way in which intellectual life as well as material life will improve after capitalism has been
abolished. The point is made that:

> capitalism is going too slow for science, that it has become a
> brake and a fetter upon Science and Technique, as it is upon all
> productive forces. (p31)

Socialism, on the other hand, will open up the prospect of a wider cultural development as well as lay the basis for a new moral attitude:

> The new generation of children will be born into a new world. The building of a free Socialist Britain will lead the whole human race towards a new world. (p46)

The same intellectual, cultural and moral advance is envisaged by the 1939 *DP*, the 1951-52 and the 1958 *BRS*. Let us just quote from the last one mentioned:

> The aim must be to give everyone access to humanity's rich store of learning and the arts, to help them to carry forward all that is best in our human and cultural traditions, to encourage them in the spirit of democracy and international brotherhood, and to enable them to go forward, swiftly and with certainty, to the building and enjoyment of a new life. (p27)

One of the merits of the 1968 and 1978 *BRS* is that they both devote a good deal of attention to the ideological and moral aspect. In the former, the opening chapter shows that, in addition to economic power and political power, the capitalist class also holds ideological power, with harmful consequences in terms of intellectual stagnation, cultural decline and moral degradation. The denunciation of this last feature is especially eloquent in the 1978 *BRS*:

> Capitalism's contradictions are not only in the sphere of economics. All human activities are seen as a source of profit. While men and women are exploited at work, their cultural, sporting and leisure activities are commercialised ... The development of science is distorted ... The economic crisis of capitalism is paralleled by a deep political, social, cultural and moral crisis. (p8)

Such a bankrupt system must be destroyed and be replaced with a new one, which will make possible the development of:

> ...a new outlook of co-operation and concern for the common good, (and) the ending of attitudes and habits associated with the class-divided society of the past. (p61)

(b) The socialist revolution
The apocalyptic view that the socialist revolution was the spectacular

storming of the enemy's fortress, Bastille or Winter Palace, may have appealed to generations of revolutionaries, but it was never that of Lenin or of the Communist Party. The expectation of what the Germans call "Der Tag" (The Day) or the French "Le Grand Soir" (The Great Evening) as the one act which would sweep clean the bourgeois mess at one fell swoop is a romantic notion that has little to do with a scientific approach to the subject. According to Lenin:

> The socialist revolution is not one single act, not one single battle on a single front, but a whole epoch of intensified class conflicts, a long series of battles on all fronts, ie battles around all the problems of economics and politics, which can culminate only in the expropriation of the bourgeoisie.[1]

Following in Lenin's footsteps, every Communist Party programme has made the same point, from the first one, which declared that the:

> ...revolution is not a single spontaneous act, coming like a bolt from the blue. It is a continuous process.(FSB,p21)

to the 1978 BRS, which stated that the revolution:

> ...will not be a single act, but the culmination of a process of struggle. (1978 BRS, p37)

The conception of revolution as a continuous process should not be confused with "gradualism," which is an attitude that the Communist movement has consistently opposed. "Gradualism" is the pet theory of reformists who claim to prefer evolution, described by them as the sensible method of doing one thing at a time, to revolution, caricatured by then as overnight instant destruction. However, what is wrong with "gradualism" is not the common-sense decision to proceed one step at a time, but the belief that at the end of the road, the capitalist system will have neatly (and willingly?) transformed itself into its opposite, socialism. But it stands to reason that no class ever commits suicide, and historical experience confirms that every obsolete social system had to be destroyed in order to make way for the new.

The process envisaged by Marxists certainly involves a series of reforms, but their value is not that they make a revolutionary break unnecessary, it is rather that they pave the way for it. In the end, they strengthen the working class to such an extent that it finds itself able to implement the ultimate "reform" – which is the revolutionary ousting of the capitalist class from power. In the words of the 1978 BRS:

> The later stages of the democratic process would, in effect, be the period of revolutionary transition to socialism. (p49)

Since the socialist revolution involves a series of steps, each leading to the next one and overlapping with it, the question of the next immediate step is one that the revolutionary party cannot evade. This is why, in addition to a long-term programme of advance, the culmination of the revolution as it were, all the programmes of the Communist party have also offered an immediate programme, Act One of the revolution in other words. The one exception is the 1935 *FSB*, which reflects the party's then belief that the time was ripe for establishing Soviet power in Britain.

Introducing the programme at the 13th party congress, R Page Arnot criticised those who imagined that "the Communist plan is for some dim, distant future" and said that such people were "blind to what has been happening in the world, nor do they understand the dreadful situation in this country today".[2] In spite of this, however, at the 1935 general election, the CPGB did not regret its 1929 demand for a "Revolutionary Workers' Government," but campaigned instead for the return of a Labour government. Such a decision, however, was not included in the party programme as part of an overall strategy.

It was left to the 1939 *DP* to become the first CPGB programme which regarded the election of a progressive Labour government as the first step on the road to socialism. The novelty did not consist in preferring a Labour government to a Tory government, for with the short exception of the "Class against Class" period this had always been the standard Communist policy, but in the unprecedented implication that the Communist Party might actually support a government which was operating under capitalism. One cannot fully appreciate the significance of this development unless one views it against the background of the experience gained by the international Communist movement during the Popular Front period. Until then, the idea that a Communist party in a capitalist country should support a non-proletarian government was regarded as thoroughly reformist. The fact that the CPGB, with Comintern approval had advocated "Vote Labour" at nearly all general elections did not mean that it was prepared to give full support to a Labour government if elected. It rather meant that it would encourage workers to put pressure on it for the satisfaction of their most pressing demands and that it believed that the experience of Labour in office would reveal in practice the limitations and the "treachery" of social-democracy.

In the summer of 1935, at the seventh Comintern congress, the issue of the Communists' attitude towards a progressive non-socialist government took on a new aspect, and in this opening speech, Dimitrov asserted that if a Popular Front government was formed "under conditions of political crises", Communists should definitely support it and might even join it. He was careful to stress that the matter would have to be decided in the light of an "actual situation" and that "no ready-made recipes could be prescribed in advance". A year later, French and Spanish Communists were faced with the historical opportunity of joining or supporting the Popular Front governments which had been formed in their respective countries. At first, the PCF fought shy of actual participation, but pledged full support. Later, it realised it had made a mistake and subsequently it offered to join the Blum government on more than one occasion, but its offers were rejected. In Spain, the mistake was not repeated, and in fact it was the Frenchman Duclos who, on the Comintern's behalf, advised Spanish Communists to enter the Frente Popular government, which they did.

There is no doubt that the evolution of the international Communist movement contributed to altering the stand of the CPGB with regard to a Labour government which the people themselves had helped to elect as a result of their own struggles. In view of its small size, it is unlikely that the CPGB would have been invited to join such a government, but while sensibly taking the view that its presence or absence "could not be laid down in advance", it added a special chapter to the 1939 *DP* in order to suggest the kind of measures an anti-fascist Labour government should carry out. None of these measures was revolutionary and none was so radical that a non-Marxist party was bound to reject it. Had not the Second World War broken out soon afterwards, the immediate programme advocated by the CPGB might have become the one to be adopted by the broad labour movement.

The next step in the CPGB's evolution was that, prior to the 1945 general election, it advocated a government of national unity, with Labour in the majority. As already pointed out, this was the result of the party's mistaken belief that the British capitalist class, having co-operated with the Soviet Union during the war, would carry that co-operation forward in peace time and would even agree – under pressure – to a number of far-reaching social reforms. Fortunately, this erroneous approach was too short lived to find its way into a party programme, but Communist historians and Communist activists should analyse the reasons for the mistake and learn from it. The very brief remarks that follow are merely a partial contribution to such a necessary analysis.

Unlike the CPGB, the Labour Party refused to contemplate a post-war coalition, probably because it had gauged the mood of the country better than the Communists. Ironically, it was the reformist LP which gave the impression of being in a fighting class mood whereas the revolutionary CP was envisaging, in the words of Harry Pollitt, that:

> ...large sections of the capitalist class themselves... will also become convinced, even if reluctantly, that such measures [eg. nationalisation – MA] are unavoidable.[3]

What was really happening was not a reversal of traditional roles but rather that the Labour leaders entered the election with the aim of taking over from the Tories in order to show that they could manage the system better than they, whereas the CPGB thought that, given the then balance of forces, national unity would best serve the interests of the working class. That such an analysis was mistaken does not alter the fact that Communists regarded the coming election and its sequels as something much more important than switching the House of Commons majority from one party to another, whilst leaving the social system basically unaffected. What was wrong was not the call for broad unity in order to tackle the problems of post-war reconstruction, but the naive belief that such unity could include "enlightened" Tories.

The culmination of the CPGB's post-war thinking on the immediate practical aim which the movement must set itself is the clear formulation of the 1978 *BRS*, viz:

> ...the winning of a new type of Labour government, which will begin to carry out a new type of left policy. (p38)

Previous editions of the *BRS* laid the ground for such a formulation, but did not actually spell it out. The 1951-52 version spoke of a "People's Government on the basis of a Parliament truly representative of the people" (p12), but although quite clear about the policies which the "People's Government" would carry out, it was rather vague as to when it was realistic to expect a sufficient number of Socialists and Communists in Parliament on whom such a government could rely. It was right to say that:

> The essential condition for ... establishing ... a people's power is the building up of a broad coalition of popular alliance of all sections of the working people ... (p13)

But it was content to leave it at that.

Its 1958 successor was a little more specific in that it pledged that:

> The Communist Party will always work for a Labour Government as against the Tories. (p13)

but it went on to warn that:

> A reformist Labour government is not the same thing as a Socialist Government which draws its strength from the mass movement of the people... (ibid)

It was, too, vague about when such a Socialist Government could be expected, and like the 1951-52 programme, it declared that:

> The development of the struggle on the immediate issues facing the people is the key to the building up of the united movement... (ibid)

The 1968 *BRS* also stated that what it called "the next stage" was the building of "a broad popular alliance around the leadership of the working class" (p28), and then it proceeded to list the various "fields of struggle" in such a way that, in effect, it put forward a programme for a progressive Labour government, but without actually mentioning it. The concluding section of the chapter entitled "Next steps ahead" is called "A People's Programme," and it declares, among other things, first, that the implementation of such a programme would be a great step forward; and secondly, that:

> In the course of the struggle new political alignments will be created... (p46)

Instead of simply saying that the struggle will create "new political alignments", which is what all its predecessors either said or implied, the 1978 *BRS* took the view that such an approach was substantially correct but not specific enough.

It therefore decided that the struggle would be strengthened if it set itself an immediately realisable goal, viz the return of a Labour government which would be committed to left policies. It justified its stand by saying that:

> It is impossible to proceed overnight from Labour governments which in effect manage capitalism to a government which introduces socialism. The political conditions for establishing socialism do not yet exist: they have to be won. Left governments are part of the process which must show the need for more fundamental change, while at the same time creating more favourable conditions for such change. (p37)

The only weakness of this otherwise excellent paragraph is that it does not explain the difference between a government "which introduces socialism" and a government which carries out socialist policies. As we shall see presently, to demand a government committed to socialist policies is not to demand "instant socialism," as revisionists are fond of saying when they try to laugh their opponents out of court, but to demand policies which make decisive inroads into capitalism. For without such policies, it is impossible to put "Britain on a new course," as the *BRS* demands. It is right and proper to call such policies "socialist," first, because they are anti-capitalist and more specifically anti-monopoly capitalist; secondly, because only socialists can actually elaborate them (though they may and should be supported by broad sections which are not consciously socialist); and finally, because their implementation would pave the way for socialism proper.

The two basic features of revolution are its socio-economic aspect and its political aspect. The socio-economic aspect was clarified by Marx when he defined a revolution as a fundamental change in existing property relations:

At a certain stage of development, the material productive forces of society come into conflict with the existing relations of production or – this merely expresses the same thing in legal terms – with the property relations within the framework of which they have operated hitherto. From forms of development of the productive forces these relations turn into their fetters. Then begins an era of social revolution.[4]

What follows from this statement is that revolutions do not happen at will, but only when there is an insoluble conflict between the productive forces, on the one hand, and social relations, on the other. Such a conflict exists today because the social character of modem production is incompatible with private ownership and the pursuit of profit. In that sense, the "era of social revolution" may be said to have started over a century ago, soon after the development of modern industry. However, the fact that the objective situation is revolutionary does not mean that capitalism will col lapse under the strain of its own contradictions, for what is needed to bring it to an end is the collective will of human beings. Lenin pointed out that a situation is fully revolutionary "only when the 'lower classes' do not want the old and when the 'upper classes' cannot continue in the old way".[5]

It was also Lenin who showed the political essence of a revolution when he wrote:

The transfer of state power from one class to another class is the first, the principal, the basic sign of a revolution, both in the strictly scientific and in the practical political meaning of the term.[6]

The fact that the revolution involves the conquest of state power by the working class and its allies has been inscribed in every Communist Party programme, from *FSB*, which declared that in order to build socialism the British working class would need to hold power in their own hands, to the latest version of the *BRS*, which stated that:

The essential feature of a socialist revolution is the winning of state power by the working class and its allies. (p36)

In recent years, however, revisionists have started to challenge what they call this "statist" conception of the revolution and to counterpose it with "self-management" by the people themselves. On this issue, as on nearly all others, the revisionists reason in an undialectical and unhistorical way. They see the formal contradiction between a central authority (the state) which is responsible for central planning, and the participation of the broad masses, but they fail to see that socialism requires the dialectical fusion of these two opposites. Moreover, they are blind to the historical experience of all existing socialist countries which shows that the winning of state power by the working class is the precondition for any kind of popular participation in the running of society. In Russia, for example, it was after the Tsarist state had been destroyed, after the winning of state power by the workers and the peasants that they were able to exercise real control over their own affairs.

It is true that the socialist countries' experience also shows that bureaucratic distortions, some of them of the utmost tragic severity, can occur when one aspect, the central authority of the state, is emphasised at the expense of the other, democratic participation. The conclusion drawn by revolutionaries is that both aspects are needed, and we shall briefly examine in the next section of this chapter the practical proposals put forward by the Communist Party in order to achieve this necessary combination. At this stage, however, there is another aspect of the "statist" argument which must be considered, viz the extent to which the Communist Party's strategy relies on the masses of the people or on a small group of dedicated revolutionaries.

Once again, one must beware of false oppositions, for there is no insuperable difficulty in combining the need for providing guidance and leadership, which is the role of a vanguard party such as the CP, and the involvement of the people. On this issue, the Communist Party has always been faithful to Lenin's dictum that:

> We are not Blanquists, we are not in favour of the seizure of power by a minority.[7]

Despite the erroneous belief that British Communists are late converts to democratic methods in achieving power, it is worth stressing that in introducing the party's very first programme, Page Arnot said that the main task of the working-class party was the "winning of the majority of the workers to its side".[8] It was therefore in line with a long-standing Communist tradition that the 1978 edition of the *BRS* could describe the party's aim as "winning the majority of the people for socialist policies" (p37).

So far we have assumed as a truism that since the Communist Party is committed to the socialist revolution, it is committed to a series of theoretical and practical campaigns which put socialism on the agenda. We are now informed by revisionists that at the present time socialism is music for the distant future and that it would be both utopian and harmful to allow it to figure as top priority on the party's agenda. When Marxist-Leninists doggedly insist that they very much want to keep socialism on the agenda, they do not mean that they expect "instant socialism" overnight. Nor do they mean that they will not work on immediate issues with people who do not share their overall view that capitalism must make way for socialism. So what does their demand mean? A concrete example will clarify the issue. Let us take the campaigns around the health service. A Communist who is taking part in the struggle to prevent the closure of a particular hospital would argue roughly along these lines: "Let us all demand, by means of petitions, demonstrations, and so on, that our hospital remains open. Nothing more to begin with. But if we are successful and if we want our victory to be secure, we have got to challenge the privatisation plans of the Tory government. Doing that means challenging a basic concept of capitalism, the concept of private property for the sake of profit. The next step is to challenge capitalism all along the line. This is what we Communists call opening up the way to socialism. When you see that this, and this alone, makes sense, we shall do the job together, just as we fought together to keep our hospital open."

Let us now look at the way in which a Labour Party committed to socialist policies would present the issue of health to the electorate. It would say roughly this: "We are not going to close down any hospitals; instead, we shall try to build many more and improve health facilities for the people. In order to achieve this, we shall need your active support, because we shall be faced with the bitter resistance of those who prefer private health to public one, in other words, the capitalists who put profits before people." Would this lose Labour any votes? Not at all, because it would not be demanding a blank cheque for socialism, but it would be explaining to the people that in order to guarantee that partial reforms are not jeopardise it is necessary to extend the fight against capitalism. Such an extension would not be decided arbitrarily by the government, but only if and when the people see the need for it. Moreover, the purpose of an election campaign is not only to win votes (although it goes without saying that this is crucial), it is also to educate and involve the people. There would be no point in being elected on the basis of a misunderstanding, ie in the belief that Labour would not touch socialism with a barge pole. Labour must explain that while its short-term programme is not socialism but inroads into the power of monopoly capital, it is ultimately committed to go much further, and will do so when the British people are ready for it.

In order to get to the guts of the argument around the issue, whether socialism is on the agenda, we have to go back at least to the period leading up to the 1983 general election and the fierce debate within the Labour Party, openly waged before an incredulous electorate, over whether Labour should commit itself to implementing conference decisions if elected, or go the country with a more "pragmatic" (ie right-wing) approach.

Although we were not realistically envisaging then that the next Labour government would be genuinely socialist (given Labour's divided though predominantly right-wing leadership and the fact that even the sum of conference decisions did not amount to a coherent socialist alternative), this pre-election argument is the basis of the debate we are having now. What it boils down to is whether or not socialists should campaign for policies which seriously threaten capitalist ideology and power.

The differences were acknowledged in the debate between Stuart Hall and Tony Benn printed in *Marxism Today* (January 1985). Hall argued that Thatcherism had established such a "hegemony" over the nation that the left was not in a position to mount the challenge of a socialist alternative indeed it should not even think about it. Tony Benn, on the other hand, focused on the fundamental character of the present capitalist crisis which lay behind the demagogy of the "New Right," and he answered the question which Hall avoided: how do we alter the existing balance of forces which we are told is so unfavourable to us? He thought that:

> The time has come when we should argue our case in our terms and not try to defend our case against arguments that are put in their terms.[9]

He added that:

> unless we offer the prospect of real change to the British people they will not support us, follow us, or elect us; and... unless we begin to make fundamental changes we shall be swept out of office very rapidly.[10]

This is a very important point, for what is involved here is a recognition that concrete alternatives do matter, that without them it is a complete waste of time going on about shifting "hegemony" and winning "converts". And the essence of this alternative needs to be spelt out: socialism.

Socialism must be on the agenda, not in terms of its being "round the corner", but because we have to show that only the implementation of socialist policies, opening up the way to socialism itself, can take us out of the present capitalist crisis. There simply is no other way. The ability to highlight the pressing need for socialism which the present capitalist crisis reveals is what distinguishes Communist leadership from reformist inertia. If we now reject a socialist alternative strategy, what alternative are we supposed to offer instead? It is difficult to see how a non-socialist alternative would not involve a lurch to the right.

Perhaps it is not so much a question of "is socialism on the agenda?" as "should socialism be on the agenda?" An agenda, unlike an objective condition, reflects the consciousness and the political priorities of those who draw it up. If the "iron" laws of history were sufficient for rolling us down the road to socialism, there would be no need for a Communist Party.

Ideas, wrote Marx, became a material force when they have "gripped the masses". But the revisionists want us to let go. That is the logic of the view that socialist policies do not need to be put on the agenda in the broad·democratic alliance against monopoly capital. For the extreme revisionists, socialism is not only off the agenda, it would take a major ideological advance to bring it up under "any other business"! For a genuine Communist Party, it is not so much "on" the agenda, it is the agenda.[11]

The last issue which must be discussed in relation to the socialist revolution is the CPGB's changing attitudes to the forms it will take. Whereas the party's views concerning the essence of the revolution-the winning of state power by the working class and its allies -never varied over the years, what it thought about its forms did change and had to change in the light of a developing historical situation. To put it in a nutshell, before the war, the CPGB was committed to violent revolution, but after the war, it took the view that a peaceful transition to socialism was possible in Britain. It is only those who confuse essence and form who accuse the party of having switched from a revolutionary to a non-revolutionary position. The truth is that the Marxist stand on the form of the revolution has always been a flexible one. A Lenin pointed out:

> Marx did not commit himself – or the future leaders of the socialist revolution – to matters of form, to methods and ways of bringing about the revolution; for the understood perfectly well that a vast number of new problems would arise...[12]

What non-Marxists are found of calling one of the party's frequent "somersaults" was therefore nothing more than the application of the Marxist method which makes it imperative for a serious political party of the working class to change its policy when the situation changes. Rather than try to decide which of the two CPGB attitudes was absolutely correct, it is more profitable to examine how each one corresponded to an existing historical situation and so was "correct" for its own time.

Before the Second World War, nobody in the Communist movement challenged the belief that the socialist revolution would be achieved by violent means and would involve an armed uprising. In fact, this was one of the key issues over which revolutionaries clashed with reformists. To the reformists' "illusion" that a peaceful path was possible, the revolutionaries opposed the "realistic" view that capitalist force must be crushed by working-class force. Admittedly, neither Marx nor Lenin had ruled out altogether the possibility of a peaceful revolution, but both had insisted that such a possibility would arise only in exceptional circumstances. In the majority of cases, however, violence would be unavoidable because, as the authors of *FSB* put it, "the capitalists are certain to resist with alr their might" (p21). After the Second World War, a number of CPs, especially those in western Europe, began to envisage (with the CPSU's blessing, be it noted) a peaceful road, not because they had come to believe in the capitalists' reasonableness, but simply because in the post-war world the balance of forces had shifted radically in favour of the working class and its allies. As a result, although the ruling class was still prepared to use force in order to defend its power and privileges, it was no longer certain that it could do so. The growth and influence of the socialist camp, and in the case of Britain, the loss of empire and the increased militancy of the British working class, all these were factors which considerably limited the capitalists' ability to use forcible methods. Before the war, such a change in the balance of forces had not taken place, and so, violent revolution was the only realistic perspective.

It is interesting to compare the way in which the issue was presented in *FSB* and in the 1939 *DP*. *FSB* insisted that "civil war is forced upon the working class" (p22), and. furthermore, unlike present-day ultra-leftists, it did not issue incantatory slogans of the "armed road the only road" type, but it rather showed that the armed road was the culmination of a manysided battle, its last step. Precisely how and when this last step would be taken was not discussed. And wisely so, for at this stage it would have been mere speculation. As for the *DP*, it avoids the prescriptive tone of its predecessor and did not say, like *FSB*, that "this overthrow must be a forceful one" (p21, my emphasis-MA), preferring to emphasise that the final decision does not rest on revolutionaries in the first place, but on those who hold power and are determined to keep it. Its approach may be summarised as follows: (a) We no not choose violence; (b) We do not know whether violence will be imposed on us; (c) We must be prepared to answer force with force. And if the *DP* denounced the "fatal illusion" that "political power can be peacefully transferred to the working class by a parliamentary majority" (p37), it must be remembered, first, that contemporary Communists also take the view that winning an election is not enough, and secondly and more importantly from a historical point of view, that the developments which occurred in the 1930s had done nothing to encourage the belief that capitalists would "play the game": they unleashed the fascist terror in Germany, they launched the civil war in Spain, they destroyed the Popular Front gains in France, and there at home, their Tory Party was returned to power in 1935 by fraudulently deceiving public opinion.

Although the issue of a peaceful road to socialism was vigorously debated in the movement at the end of the war, as can be seen from the writings of Pollitt and others, strangely enough, it was not mentioned as such in the first edition of the *BRS*. The 1951-52 document rejected the lie that communism needs a world war in order to be "imposed", but it did not actually speak of averting civil war. The nearest it came to suggesting a peaceful path was the statement that:

The path forward for the British people will be to establish a

People's Government on the basis of a Parliament truly representative of the people. (p12)

A little further down, the 1951-52 *BRS* warned that:

It would be wrong to believe that the big capitalists will voluntarily give up their property and their big profits in the interests of the British people.

It would be more correct to expect them to offer active resistance to the
decisions of the People's Government, and to fight for the retention of their
privileges by all means in their power, including force.

Therefore the British people and the People's Government
should be ready to rebuff such attempts. (p15)

The 1958 *BRS* was published after the international Communist movement
had spectacularly endorsed the peaceful road as a distinct possibility for
some capitalist countries, and so, it is not surprising that it came out more
forcefully in favour of the idea. In particular, it listed the most important
factors which strengthen the possibility of a peaceful road in Britain, viz the
fact that "more than a third of the world's population has already taken the
socialist road", which means that we would not have "to face single-handed
a hostile capitalist encirclement" (p10); "the increasing strength of the working class and progressive movement throughout the world" (ibid); and finally, the existence in this country of a "powerful labour movement [which]
embodies the British workers' fighting ability" and of "strong traditions of
democratic institutions" (ibid). However, "peaceful" is not synonymous
with "conflict-free". Quite the reverse, for the next step, the election of a Labour and Communist majority, will take place "at a time of mounting class
struggle" (ibid). With regard to the predictable resistance on the part of the
big capitalists, the 1958 *BRS* did not in the least forget it, but rather expected
that the enemy would use all means, "constitutional and unconstitutional"
to hold back the popular movement. The main thing, however, was that:
The extent to which the working class is alert and prepared to use its
strength in support of the government's measures will determine whether
the big capitalists accept the democratic verdict of the people or attempt to
resist by force. (p11)
Whereas the first versions of the *BRS* were either silent or brief on the
issue of the peaceful road to socialism, the 1968 *BRS* devoted a special section to it under the title "By Peaceful Means." The urgent need to clarify as
much as possible the meaning of the peaceful transition envisaged by the
CPGB was no doubt due to the polemics with the Maoists, but it was also
a response to the misgivings and the criticisms expressed by a number of

party members. First of all, the 1968 *BRS* rejected the view that "peaceful" means "without a struggle". All it means is "without civil war":

> It is in the best interests of the working people... that this mass struggle for political power should be carried through by peaceful means, without civil war. (p48)

The peaceful road does not represent a pacifist pledge that force will never be used under any circumstances, but the assertion that the working class and its allies aim to come to power without an armed uprising. Far from implying that the path will be smooth and easy, the CPGB programme sharply warned that "these developments, this programme will have to be fought for by the mass movement at every step..." (p49)

Secondly, coming to power "by peaceful means" does not, of itself, guarantee that force will not be used. The success of the peaceful road depends on the strength of the working class, and also on its ability and readiness to use every form of struggle, including violence if and when it proves necessary.

Thirdly, the 1968 *BRS* did not tell the British people that they could bank on the certainty of peaceful revolution, but that "this is a perspective that can be achieved... at a time of mounting class struggle, when the over whelming majority of the people is in action". (p50)

Fourthly, the *BRS* based its confidence on the fact that in this country, the labour movement is strong and that there is a growing number of non-working class people who are ready "to assist in developing socialism" (ibid).

Finally, the ruling class cannot launch a civil war unless there are people who are ready to do the fighting on its behalf. The process of political education which is involved in the building of a broad popular alliance, and which the *BRS* repeatedly advocated, will reduce the chances of misguided sections answering any call for violence, whether such a call is inspired by fascist organisations or by other forces.

Moreover, the democratisation of the armed forces, also demanded by the 1968 *BRS*, should make it more difficult for the ruling class to use the army against the people. The only criticism which can be made of the section entitled "By Peaceful Means" is that it did not mention the international factors which can contribute to the peaceful development of the socialist revolution in Britain. On this point, Dave Priscott had this to say:

> Civil war has all too often been interventionist war; the changing balance of world forces makes this an increasingly risky gamble for imperialism. If the USA today cannot defeat Vietnam, what hopes are there for them to try it on with us, in a few years time, when all the internal antagonisms of American

society will have grown still sharper and when the socialist world will be still stronger?[13]

Dave Priscott was writing at the beginning of 1972. About a year and a half later, the fascist coup in Chile seemed to have dashed all hopes that a peaceful transition to socialism was a practical possibility: Allende came to power by constitutional means but before he was allowed to carry out a programme of far-reaching reforms (not even socialist ones), reactionary officers, backed by the USA, staged a military coup against him, murdered him, and replaced him with the fascist butcher General Pinochet. Didn't this prove that the peaceful road leads to an impasse and to tragedy?

This is obviously not the place to attempt a detailed analysis of the Chilean experience, but in so far as it is relevant to the peaceful road advocated by the 1968 *BRS*, one important lesson that can be drawn from it is that the success of any road to socialism depended on the vigilance of the working class, on its ability not to be cut off from its real allies, and finally on its readiness to use all forms of struggle as and when the situation demands it.

The 1978 *BRS* came out after the Chilean counter-revolution, and in the light of this, it did not rule out the possibility of a right-wing armed coup against a left government. It rather discussed in a serious way in the last section of chapter 3, "Meeting capitalist resistance." It began by warning that the ruling class would use legal as well as illegal methods. The legal battle would be mainly conducted by the Tory Party, but the Tories would not benefit from pluralism, provided the left government had succeeded in:

> ...winning the support of the majority of the people, taking them into its confidence, and extending their democratic rights. (p48)

The illegal battle might take the form of an armed coup. If such a coup was attempted:

> ...the government should have no hesitation in using force to defeat it, and mobilising the full strength of the working class and progressive movement to defend democracy. (ibid)

One important issue the 1978 *BRS* did not shirk was the role of the armed forces. It made the valid point that a non-violent revolution was impossible unless these were neutralised, if not indeed won over to the cause of the labour movement. In order to achieve this, the CPGB programme advocated democratising the armed forces, and trying to win direct political support from them.

It is worth noting that on the crucial issue of the forms of the socialist revolution in Britain, the 1978 *BRS* avoids both the dogmatic assertion of the ultra-left that violence is inevitable and the no less dogmatic assertion of the social-democrats that "social peace" is guaranteed by our institutions and our democratic traditions.

Instead, we are told in the clearest possible terms that "a coup is neither inevitable nor impossible," because the whole thing "depends primarily on the relation of political forces" (p49). Revolutionaries cannot and must not promise in advance that this or that would happen. They can only put forward their assessment of what is both possible and desirable, and conclude, as does the *BRS*, that the final outcome is up to the people.

(c) Socialist society

Concerning the economic basis of socialism, there is a remarkable continuity throughout all Communist Party programmes. They all agree that its two main features are nationalisation which would apply to the big firms only and that a small private sector is not incompatible with the socialist (as distinct from communist) stage of social development. The most significant change in the party's evolution concerns the issue of compensation for the former owners of nationalised industries. The two pre-war programmes are adamant that there would be no compensation. Thus *FSB* asserts that British soviets "will take over, without compensation, the banks, the big factories, the mines, the transport concerns, etc. from their present owners". (p29) And the *DP* speaks of "nationalisation without compensation of all large private capitalist enterprises... and of all landed estates". (p42) On the other hand, the post-war *BRS* programmes offer limited compensation. In the 1951-52 it is said that:

> ...there will be partial compensation to those who do not resist the policy of the People's Government, but no compensation to those who resist the People's Government. (p15)

From 1958 onwards, the Communist Party programmes envisage "reasonable" compensation in the form of life annuities to individuals. (See 1958 *BRS*, p18, 1968 *BRS*, p57, and 1978 *BRS*, p51)

With regard to planning, all the programmes state that its purpose is to ensure the satisfaction of the people's needs. The people's involvement at local and central level is mentioned in *FSB*, the *DP*, and the successive versions of the *BRS*, and reference is made to the role of the co-operative movement and to the new responsibilities of trade unions under socialism. The 1968 *BRS* shows itself aware of "the dangers of over-centralisation of planning" and says that they "could be avoided by wide consultation, not only in the preparation of plans, but also in carrying them out". (p59)

On the question of finance, the stand taken by the first party programme has remained that of the Communist Party with only minor changes of emphasis or of presentation. *FSB* declared that the question, "Where is the money to come from this whole programme?" was based on a misunderstanding:

> Money is only a means of exchanging things. What matters is the things which are made by human labour. When all are working there will be an increase in the quantity of food, raw materials, manufactured goods, etc. It is these which will be used to raise the standard of living, housing and social services. (p41)

This is not substantially different from what the 1978 *BRS* says:

> The financial policy of a socialist government would be a means of ensuring proper use of the country's resources, labour, plant, materials and the land ... Budget expenditure would include funds for expanding socially desirable production and for all social services.

Turning now to the social aspects of socialism, again, we notice a remarkable continuity in describing socialist society as one which affords human beings basic rights ignored by capitalism, such as the right to work, to leisure, to health, housing, and so on; a high standard of culture, with the unprecedented development of art and science; and a new sense of dignity. The most significant changes are those which affect women, the youth, and black people, not so much because of the greater attention paid to them, largely as a result of the importance these issues have acquired in recent years.

On women, the Communist Party's constant attitude has been that it stood for complete equality between the sexes, but apart from making this position abundantly clear, most programmes before 1968 and especially 1978 did not examine the issue in any great detail. In the 1968 *BRS*, the paragraph demanding equal rights and opportunities for women stressed that these:

> ...are not only a matter of justice, but would bring great benefits to the country in all spheres of work and activity. (p40)

It is, however, one of the great merits of the 1978 *BRS* that it goes beyond these general statements. Women are mentioned three times, first as one of the new social forces (pp29-30), next as one of the democratic issues which must be tackled by a left Labour government (p42), and finally, as a group which has a special role and special demands under socialism (pp59-60). In the section "Social forces and movements," the *BRS* acknowledges its debt to the women's liberation movement, saying that it "has been a major stimulus to thought and action", "has focused attention on the sexual division of labour", and has "raised other questions on the nature of personal relationships, human sexuality, and the future of the family" (p30).

Let us also note that the same section welcomes the development of the gay movement and that the Communist Patty was the first political party in Britain to denounce anti-gay prejudice. To those in the labour movement who think, and even openly say that none of this concerns the working class, the *BRS* replies that the women's struggle in particular "is an integral part of the struggle for socialism" (p29). Communists are and should be very much concerned with the fight to end all forms of sexual discrimination because socialism represents liberation from all the evils of capitalism and class societies, including liberation from sexual prejudices, from domineering and patronising attitudes, and from any sort of behaviour which degrades human beings.

Although the *BRS* emphasises that socialism alone would bring liberation to women and the blacks, it warns that the winning of state power by the working class and its allies and the building of a socialist system in economic and political fields would be only a beginning. It reminds us that the ending of legal and economic discrimination against women in existing socialist countries is a most important achievement, but that these countries "still have to conduct a constant battle against outworn ideas carried over from the past". (p60) The same point is made about racism because "ideas and prejudices linger on in society long after the material basis for them has been abolished". (p57) Hence the need for a socialist society to conduct a "vigorous ideological campaign" against racist prejudices. AB for young people, they would benefit from the greater opportunities which socialism offers in all areas, but the *BRS* shows that in this field as well there would be no automatic advance without an ideological struggle, if only because of the deplorable "historic neglect of young people by the labour and progressive movement" (p33).

Turning now to the political aspects of socialist society, the three issues which require discussion are the dictatorship of the proletariat, the role of Parliament, and pluralism. The dictatorship of the proletariat was the name given by Marx to working-class power, to the special kind of state which the workers must set up immediately after they take power. He called it a dictatorship because, to him, all forms of state represented the dictatorship of a class – the class which, having force and the law on its side, can dictate its will to the rest of society. Lenin, who endorsed and applied Marx's concept, explained why, in the period immediately following the abolition of capitalism, the state had to be in the hands of a single class: it was unthinkable, he asserted, that other classes apart from the working class (the Russian peasantry, for example) would set themselves socialist aims before the revolution; this could only happen after they had seen socialism work out in practice.

At the second Comintern congress in 1920, one of the 21 conditions for joining the new International was acceptance of the dictatorship of the proletariat, and right up to the end of the Second World War, such acceptance had been a common feature to all Communist parties. When the concept of "People's Democracy" was put forward in the late 1940s and early 1950s, a new chapter began. At first, all that the Communists of Eastern Europe claimed was that "people's democracy" was different from the soviet form of government, but that in essence, it fulfilled all the functions of the dictatorship of the proletariat under new conditions. Later, however, a great number of CPs in capitalist countries no longer included the dictatorship of the proletariat in their programmes and justified this by saying that the word "dictatorship" had been given sinister connotations by the fascist dictators, and that it was therefore better to express the Communists' commitment to working-class power without using the phrase "dictatorship of the proletariat".

Eventually, it became clear that the issue was not only one of terminology, but of political content. As far as the CPGB was concerned, it issued an important statement in November 1976 which, after recalling that for Marx, Engels and Lenin, the dictatorship of the proletariat represented genuine democracy for the masses of the people, went on to explain why in the new party programme then in the process of being drafted, the phrase would not be used:

> First, we consider the word "dictatorship" completely inappropriate as a description of the Socialist society we want to build, and our concept is the direct opposite of the connotations it has acquired in the present century, especially as a result of the rise of fascism.
>
> Second, in this century it has become historically associated with the concept of achieving Socialism through armed insurrection, and with the specific forms, including the Soviets and the one-party system, in which Socialism was built in the Soviet Union.
>
> These are not our perspectives.
>
> Third, although Marx, Engels, Lenin all made clear that the dictatorship of the proletariat was an alliance between the working class and its allies, the term itself does not make this clear.
>
> The word "proletariat" is often taken to mean the traditional core of the working class, the industrial manual workers.
>
> Thus, the term could imply, to contemporary readers, a dicta-

> torship of this core over the rest of the population which again
> is not our position. For these reasons we do not consider it ap-
> propriate to use the term in our programme. (14)

At about the same time, other CPs were taking a similar stand and were giving their own explanations. The French Communist Party, for example, pointed out that one of the differences between the present situation and that which existed when Lenin was alive was that in Western countries a number of non-proletarian groups had already taken a pro-socialist stand. They knew from their own experience of capitalism that socialism alone would solve their problems, so that it was no longer a question of having to win them over after the revolution.

To return to the CPGB, its evolution on this issue can best be seen from the way its successive programmes described working-class power. In the pre-war ones, the word "dictatorship" was not shunned, but "proletariat" was, probably because it did nor sound very English! The 1929 manifesto demanded a "revolutionary workers' government, exercising a working class dictatorship and operating a real workers' democracy" (p6). *FSB*, as we already know, had a whole section entitled "Workers Dictatorship is Democracy for the Workers" (pp23-29), in the course of which it declared among other things that what "this dictatorship of the workers" will "mean in practice" is, first, that the capitalists will be deprived of their owner-ship of the means of production, secondly, that they will be deprived of their "liberty" to poison people's minds through their newspapers, thirdly, that they "will have their monopoly of the best halls and premises taken from them" (p28), fourthly, that they will be deprived of their monopoly of transport and travel facilities, and lastly, that they will be deprived of their "monopoly of the best means of education and culture" (ibid.) As for the 1939 *DP*, it described what it also called "the dictatorship of the working class" as involving the following: "disarm the exploiters, put an end to their armed organisations and machinery of coercion, and deprive them of politi-cal rights, so that they cannot harm the work of socialist construction and endeavour to win back power". (pp38-39)

In the post-war editions of the *BRS*, the word "dictatorship" was dropped altogether and was replaced by "People's Democracy" in the 1951-52 text, by "working-class power" in the 1958 text, and by "socialist government" in both the 1968 and 1978 versions. What is more interesting than the use of labels is the increasing attention from 1958 onwards to the measures which are needed against bureaucracy under socialism. The 1958

BRS put forward a series of democratic measures which would ensure "participation of the people in running the country" (p23), but it did not di-rectly confront the problem of the fight against bureaucracy. All that it said on the subject in its first chapter was that:

Socialism does not mean the levelling down of standards. Nor does it bring bureaucracy and tyranny. (p8)

When one recalls that this was written shortly after the 20th CPSU congress had revealed that in the socialist Soviet Union there had been bureaucracy and tyranny under Stalin, one must admit that this short sentence was quite inadequate. It might have been better to have made a brief reference to the fact that Stalin's methods were alien to socialism and to have recalled that they were denounced by the Soviet Communists themselves. There is no reason why this should not have been included in the 1968 and 1978 versions of the *BRS*, as it would have strengthened the case both of them put forward in favour of socialist democracy, a democracy which the 1978 *BRS* describes as one which depends "on the extent to which the people themselves exercise control in every area of economic, political and social life" (p58).

On the question of Parliament, there is again a radical difference between the pre-war programmes and the post-war ones. The former envisaged its abolition under socialism, whereas the latter spoke of the need to "transform" it. Actually, the 1929 manifesto being ostensibly an election programme, did not demand the abolition of Parliament in so many words. Its final section, "Political Democracy" stated that real democracy was "possible only under a system of workers' councils" (p32), but it then went on to demand:

(1) The abolition of the monarchy and the House of Lords.

(2) The adoption of a national system of proportional representation.

(3) Full political rights for soldiers, sailors, airmen, police and civil servants. (ibid)

FSB was much more explicit:

What kind of Government will the British workers establish when Capitalism has been overthrown? They will not maintain the present parliamentary system. (p23)

The programme then expressed its confidence that the British working class "will create" and "is certain to set up" (both expressions were used, the first one more than once) the workers' councils which will replace Parliament. Only once did the tone become prescriptive, viz :

These Councils or Soviets are the form of Government... which the British workers must set up." (p29, my emphasis MA).

The emphasis in *FSB* was so much on participatory rather than representative democracy that only a brief reference was made to a national authority (the equivalent of the Supreme Soviet in the USSR), whose job would be to "carry on the Government as a whole" (p25).

The 1939 *DP* repeated the case against Parliament and made the additional point that even if the representatives of the working class won a parliamentary majority, the capitalists would resort to "the most violent resistance" against a government which, based on that majority, endeavoured to "make serious inroads into the foundations of capitalist exploitation," and it would soon become necessary to create "a new type of State", having workers' councils as its basis. The most important difference between the 1935 *FSB* and the 1939 *DP* on this issue is that the latter, drawing upon the experience of the Popular Front period, envisaged a positive role for Parliament in the struggle against fascism, as has already been mentioned.

The anti-Parliament stand of the CPGB's pre-war programmes reflects the then current belief among all Communists that Parliament was a bourgeois institution. At best, it could be used by revolutionaries as a platform from which to denounce the evils of capitalism, but there would be no further use for it under socialism. This attitude is associated with the name of Lenin, but it would be wrong to imagine that he invented it, for he merely extended the views put forward by Marx and Engels and applied them to the situation as he saw it. With regard to soviets, Lenin did not regard them as constituting the abolition of representative institutions, but as their transformation. In his classic study, *The State and Revolution*, he wrote:

> The way out of parliamentarianism is not, of course, the abolition of the representative institutions and the electoral principle, but the conversion of the representative institutions from mere "talking shops" into working bodies.[15]

Moreover, soviets were an original creation of the Russian working class and peasantry. They were not set up artificially but arose spontaneously in the course of three revolutions, 1905, February 1917 and October 1917, as alternatives to the Tsarist Dumas which provided very little opportunity for the expression of popular views.

It was a serious mistake on the part of European Communists to have overlooked this last aspect, and perhaps Lenin himself must take a share of the blame. Not that he expected an exact reproduction of the Russian experience (he often said that this was neither likely nor desirable), but it is a fact that he urged western workers to set up alternative organs of power and that he confidently expected that they would do so. It is difficult to know whether he would have clung to this belief if he had not died in 1924, and it is quite possible that his realism might have convinced him that there was no evidence that councils of workers and peasants would arise spontaneously in western Europe. (Even the Councils of Action set up during the

General Strike in Britain were never meant to take the place of the House of Commons.) Be that as it may, Lenin's successors, including the authors of *FSB*, went on expecting that, without much prompting, the workers of all countries would set up their own soviets.

A number of modern Communists in the West take the view that such an expectation was unrealistic. For example, in Britain, Monty Johnstone asserted that the "Soviet road" was never suited to this country because it involved:

> ...the transformation of the forms of revolutionary struggle and power that had shown themselves suited to Russia to the very different conditions of Britain.[16]

In partial defence of *FSB*, one must point out that in pre-fascist times, parliamentary democracy was not just one of the ways by which the ruling class exercised power, but the only one, so that an attack on capitalist rule was bound to be an attack on capitalist parliamentary democracy. It is easy, with hindsight, to declare that such an attack should have focused on the limitations of the parliamentary system and should have demanded its transformation rather than its abolition, but perhaps it was necessary for the movement to go through the tragic experience of fascism before it could tackle the issue in that way. In any case, the behaviour of capitalist governments, including the British government, was hardly likely to inspire confidence in the system, so that, quite irrespective of Communist propaganda, there was a growing disillusionment with Parliament among the people. Finally, Monty Johnstone himself did not condemn pre-war Communist policy as having been entirely negative. He wrote that:

> What was relevant and positive in the Communist Party's early strategy was the rejection of the social democratic con ception of a purely parliamentary road and the emphasis on socialist revolution the bourgeois state by a new type of work ing class state power, which would be used against all attempts by the defeated capitalist minority undemocratically to defy the wishes of the people.[17]

What led the CPGB to alter its stand on Parliament after the war? That other CPs in the West were also reassessing their attitude has led unfriendly critics to declare that they were all obeying the instructions of "Moscow". Why "Moscow" should need a re-evaluation of parliamentarianism it is difficult to see, but there is, however, a very tiny grain of truth in the critics' "explanation". The CPGB was not alone in revising its approach because the war had sharply revealed to all Communists and all democrats how important it was to be clear about the specific conditions in their own country. A deeper study of British history, past and present, led the CPGB to appreciate five important facts.

The first one was that Parliament is "the product of Britain's historic struggle for democracy" (1951 *BRS*, p14), and because of this, is not a static institution, but one which has constantly evolved in the past and can evolve further still in the future. As the first *BRS* put it, it is possible to transform it "into the democratic instrument of the will of the vast majority of the people". (ibid)

The second one was that the will of Parliament lay, not in its existence, but in the way in which it was used by the ruling class to give a cloak of legality to its anti-working class actions. Hence the demand which is found in all versions of the *BRS* that Parliament should be "transformed". In the 1968 *BRS*, a few aspects of what such transformation would involve are given. For example, the House of Commons would become:

> ...a real national forum as well as a decision making body, debating statements of policy as well as voting upon Bills, drawing on the views of all relevant public organisations in discussing particular issues. It would have standing committees to enable individual members to learn about and influence administrative policies, so that these were constantly brought under public scrutiny. (p52)

The 1968 *BRS* also stressed that what was even more important than the control of the government by MPs was the control of MPs by the people. It thought it crucial to have a mass movement outside Parliament to put pressure on the House of Commons and to ensure that its decisions are upheld. In the light of this approach, it would be quite misleading to describe the *BRS* strategy as a "parliamentary road to socialism". It is rather a road of mass struggles in the course of which Parliament would be one of the institutions to be used, together with trade unions and other democratic organisations set up by the people.

The third fact was that Parliament is elected by universal suffrage and cannot be regarded in the same way as other branches of the state machine, such as the armed forces, the police, the Civil Service, and so on, over which the people have no control whatsoever. At the same time, no version of the *BRS* claimed that the existing electoral system was fair and democratic. For example, the demand for proportional representation was included in the very first *BRS* and has been maintained in all successive editions.

The fourth fact was that in this country there is an accepted convention that Parliament is sovereign, so that it is very difficult for the capitalists openly to challenge the decisions of a progressive parliamentary majority. As we already saw in connection with the CPGB's stand on the issue of the peaceful transition to socialism, no version of the *BRS* ever put forward the naive view that the ruling class could be expected to accept passively the people's democratic verdict. What every edition rather stressed was that" the resistance of the overthrown exploiters was bound to be vicious and desperate, but that it could be defeated if a united labour movement, deter mined and vigilant, made use of every single democratic channel already in existence. The sovereignty of Parliament was seen as being one of such channels.

The final fact which led the CPGB to revise its views on Parliament was the difference between Russia's and Britain's historical experience.

Whereas soviets were set up as the result of the initiative of the Russian people, the initiative of the British working class had already led to count-less forms of organisations (trade unions, co-operatives, trades councils, shop stewards' committees and so on), so that it was unnecessary to lay down in advance that a new one, soviets, simply had to be created.

Let us now briefly examine the issue of pluralism as it is tackled by suc-cessive Communist Party programmes. In the Communist vocabulary, the word "pluralism" expresses the view that a socialist society would not be a one-party regime, but one which allowed the existence of many parties, including those which were hostile to socialism. What is at stake is not whether the CP rules alone, as in the USSR or as part of a coalition, as in Eastern Europe, but whether socialism can tolerate the existence of opposi-tion parties.

In the pre-war programmes, it was taken for granted that there was no room for opposition parties under socialism for the simple reason that op-position to socialism could only come from the capitalist class and that the whole purpose of the revolution was to deprive that class of all power.

FSB, as we saw earlier, did not even bother to discuss pluralism. In *FSB*, it said:

> ...power will be in the hands of the working class, led by its most class-conscious section, organised in the Communist Par-ty... (p42)

The same view was taken by the 1939 *DP* which, in addition, specifically spelt out that the dictatorship of the working class would deprive the ex-ploiters of political rights (p39).

There was no mention of pluralism in the 1951-52 *BRS*, but one of its novel features was the implication that the People's Government which would lead Britain along the road of "People's Democracy" would be based on a Labour-Communist coalition. This is not stated in so many words, but the *BRS* declared that in order to win a progressive parliamentary majority:

> ...the united action of all sections of the working-class move-ment-Labour, trade union, co-operative and Communist is the

vital need. (p16)

One might argue that mention of a parliamentary majority implies the existence of a parliamentary minority, presumably made up of all parties hostile to socialism, but apart from this implication there was no reference in the 1951-52 *BRS* to the fate of a political opposition under socialism.

The first step in the direction of pluralism was taken by the 1958 *BRS*, in its section on "Socialist Democracy." After saying that the political organisations on which socialism depended were the "Labour Party and the Communist Party, working together for their socialist aims" (p23), the CPGB programme declared:

> At the same time the right of other political parties to maintain their organisations, party publications and propaganda, and to take part in elections, will be maintained provided that these parties conform to the law. (ibid)

The 1968 *BRS* made the same point, also in the section called "Socialist Democracy," but it was more specific than its predecessor and spoke of all "democratically organised political parties, including those hostile to socialism" (p52). It was the first time that the CPGB had committed itself to pluralism so forcefully but such a commitment in the *BRS* did not at all mean that the party was unanimous on the issue. In 1968, the debate was particularly topical – and heated – because of the Czechoslovak crisis. The April 1968 Action Programme adopted by the CPCz did not actually include pluralism as such, but it came very close to it when it pledged that the law would guarantee "the freedom of speech of minority interests and opinions".(lS) After the military intervention, those who supported the action of the Warsaw Pact countries claimed that it was this kind of misguided "bourgeois liberalism" which had encouraged counter-revolutionaries and justified the intervention. The critics of the intervention replied that the CPCz Action Programme explicitly recognised that reactionaries might "abuse the process of democratisation"[19] which meant that the party and the state were quite prepared to deal adequately with such abuses.

In the 1978 *BRS* the CPGB's commitment to pluralism was reasserted, again in a section entitled "Socialist Democracy," and the reasons for the party's stand were given. These included the fact that "classes would not immediately disappear with the establishment of socialism" (p56) and that mistaken class conceptions would be "fought politically" rather than administratively, and furthermore the realisation that:

> ...even after class divisions are eliminated the need would continue for the expression of differing political alternatives and priorities ... Such conflicts in a fully developed socialist society

would not, of course, reflect irreconcilable antagonisms as in capitalist society. (ibid)

The issue of pluralism is especially controversial when the concept is discussed in relation to a socialist society rather than to the transitional period which precedes it and leads to it. Even anti-pluralists concede that during the transitional period, say, after the united left had won a parliamentary majority, pluralism would be a fact of life – not to be welcomed, perhaps, but to be reckoned with. It is a different kettle of fish when we are dealing with a government which has already succeeded in depriving the capitalists of their economic power by taking away their firms and nationalising them. Should such a government also deprive the capitalists of their political rights? On this issue, there are deep divisions within the CPGB, but the dividing line is not between Eurocommunists and Marxist-Leninists, because pluralism has its defenders among the latter and is not confined to those who follow the revisionist line of the CPGB leadership. For this reason, we shall end this chapter by examining very briefly, and as objectively as possible, the pros and cons of the argument.

The case against pluralism rests on four propositions. First, it is at variance with the experience of all existing socialist countries. Secondly, it amounts to legalising counter-revolution since it gives the enemies of socialism a chance to mobilise against the regime. Thirdly, a commitment to pluralism in advance disarms the working class by sowing illusions about the capitalists' willingness to respect the law. Finally, the banning of opposition parties must not be seen as something decreed from above, but as a sign of the people's determination not to put the clock back after the socialist revolution.

The advocates of pluralism reject all these arguments. First, they argue that if pluralism is unprecedented it is because the peaceful path to socialism is itself unprecedented. It involves coercion of the enemy by law, not by force, by methods of persuasion and education, not by administrative means. Secondly, pluralism does not legalise counter-revolution since it carries with it the important proviso that anti-socialist parties must respect the law, the socialist law. Thirdly, a commitment to pluralism does not sow illusions among the workers: both the 1968 and the 1978 *BRS* go out of their way to warn that we must be prepared to defeat capitalist resistance by every means, including force if necessary. Finally, it is unlikely that the British people would themselves demand the banning of opposition par ties. With their age-long democratic traditions, they are more likely to withdraw their confidence from political parties which outlaw their opponents.

NOTES

1 Lenin, *Selected Works* vol 5 p268
2 R Page Arnot, Preface to *FSB*, p5
3 Harry Pollitt, *Answers to Questions* (CP, 1945, pp45-46)
4 Karl Marx, *Preface to Critique of Political Economy*
5 Lenin, "Left-wing' Communism", in *Selected Works* vol 10, p127
6 Lenin, "Letters on Tactics", in *Selected Works*, vol 6 p33
7 Lenin, "April Theses" in *Selected Works* vol 6 p29
8 R Page Arnot, op cit p5
9 Tony Benn, *Marxism Today* January 1985) p12
10 Ibid
11 Victor Adereth's contribution to these arguments is acknowledged here.
12 Lenin, *Selected Works* vol 7, p368.
13 Dave Priscott in *Marxism Today* January 1972, p31.
14 CPGB EC Statement of 14 November 1976.
15 Lenin, *State and Revolution*, Chapter 3, section 3, "The abolition of parlia-mentarism".
16 Monty Johnstone, "Early Communist Strategy: An Assessment", in *Marxism Today* (September 1978) p293
17 Ibid
18 "CPCz Action Programme", in *Marxism Today* (July 1968) p209.
19 Ibid

4

Internationalism

The internationalist character of the Communist Party expresses itself in three ways – first, in the stand it takes on foreign policy issues, especially that of war and peace; secondly, in its long-standing opposition to British imperialism and its support of national-liberation movements everywhere, especially those waged by former British colonies; and lastly, in its solidarity with other progressive forces, especially the international Communist movement and the socialist countries. Let us examine how each aspect is dealt with in successive party programmes.

With regard to foreign policy, it is a fact that the British labour movement tended to pay little attention to it in the past, believing (in the heyday of British imperialism) that all that was urgently needed as far as British workers were concerned was the solution of the so-called "social question" in Britain. The fact that the movement now recognises that it must have a different foreign policy to that of the Tories and that international affairs constitute an arena of the class struggle as important as issues of home policy is largely due to the untiring propaganda of Marxist groups before the First World War and of the CPGB since 1920. As a Marxist-Leninist party, the Communist Party does not content itself with showing the importance of foreign policy; it goes further and reveals the class character of other parties' stand on foreign affairs as well as the class character of its own alternative programme. It never fails to point out that the foreign policies of capitalist parties are designed to uphold the interests of British capitalists against their foreign capitalist rivals and – more importantly – against national-liberation movements and the socialist countries. Communist foreign policies, on the other hand, are designed to strengthen the working class, to assist national-liberation movements and to support the socialist countries. Above all, in the present period, the contrast is between capitalist foreign policy based on the arms race and the threat of war, on the one hand, and Communist foreign policy which sets itself the aims of disarmament and peace, on the other hand.

The attack on capitalism as a system which breeds war can be found in all Communist Party programmes, but the particular war threat against which the movement had to fight was not always the same. In 1929, it was the CPGB's view that "the war danger develop(ed) in two principal directions" (p30), against the USSR and against rival imperialist powers. After declaring that "war can only be eliminated by the elimination of capitalism" (p31), the 1929 manifesto went on to say that the CPGB "prepares the workers in every possible way to answer imperialist war with the class war, and the liberation war of the colonial masses" (ibid).

In *FSB*, the emphasis was on the fact that "the capitalists are driving to war," this sentence being in fact the title of one of the sections of the programme's first chapter. The point was made that when capitalism reaches the monopoly stage, ie when it becomes imperialism, "war is inevitable – unless stopped by the workers" (p17). Although the following section was entitled "The capitalists are driving to fascism," the threat of war represented by the aggressive policies of Hitler and Mussolini was not mentioned. Instead, the workers were warned that it was not only Mosley's Blackshirt gangs which were preparing for fascism, but the National Government as well.

In the 1939 *DP*, the aggressive nature of the fascist powers, Germany, Italy and Japan, was said to have led to a series of wars which were nothing but "the initial stages of the second imperialist war for the redivision of the world" (p32). The document went on to say that "in this war the aggressor powers are the fascist powers", but that "the success of their aggression (had) been made possible by the connivance of the most reactionary sections of monopoly capital in Britain and France, whose aim has been to promote a fascist war against the Soviet Union" (ibid).

At the end of the *DP*, in the chapter devoted to "The immediate programme," the demand was put forward for a "Peace Pact of Britain, France and the Socialist Soviet Union, together with all other states prepared to collaborate in the collective maintenance of peace against aggression..." (p64).

The second world war had barely ended when the threat of a third world war began to loom on the horizon, and it was against this danger that all the versions of the *BRS* issued a serious warning. For, in the words of the earliest one:

> A third world war, waged with atomic weapons, would annihilate our major cities, blot out millions of our population, and

throw Britain back for centuries. It could only end in a dreadful catastrophe for the British people. (1951 *BRS*, p8)

In order to avoid such a catastrophe, all the programmes urged the formation of the broadest possible movement for peace and disarmament. In addition, they all put forward a series of practical demands. These included the severance of Britain's links with the imperialist USA – the main source of war since 1945 – the dissolution of all military blocs such as NATO (which would bring about the end of the defensive Warsaw Pact), Britain's withdrawal from SEATO, CENTO "and other such alliances which have nothing to do with the defence of Britain" (1968 *BRS*, p37), campaign for disarmament, including Britain's unilateral renunciation of nuclear weapons (advocated in both the 1968 and the 1978 versions), the withdrawal of British troops from other countries and of all foreign (mainly US) troops from Britain, and support for the peace initiatives of the Soviet Union. Finally, a feature which is common to all the versions of the *BRS* is the assertion that "the danger of war arises from monopoly capitalism" (1968 *BRS*, p35).

It is worth noting that in the 1978 *BRS*, the demand that Britain should withdraw from NATO is not something for the dim, distant future, but is part of the measures which a left Labour government should implement as soon as it comes to power. In other words, it is something for which the labour movement must fight now. This is what the 1978 *BRS* says:

> Britain should pursue an independent foreign policy... It should campaign for detente and the fulfilment of the Helsinki Agreements, withdraw from NATO, and work for an agreed dissolution of both NATO and the Warsaw Pact and their replacement by an all-inclusive European Security System...(p4)

Another common feature is the assertion that war is not inevitable and that peaceful coexistence is possible. The point was made as early as 1951:

> The Communist Party rejects the "theory" of the inevitability of war between the Socialist and capitalist camps. On the contrary, it declares that the peaceful co-existence of Socialism and capitalism is possible, on the basis of mutual respect for national rights and independence. (pp5-6)

This position was not repudiated by any subsequent edition of the *BRS*. One must add, however, that at no time did the CPGB suggest that peaceful coexistence, disarmament and the elimination of the war threat would be achieved without struggle. In the words of the 1968 *BRS*:

> A third world war is not inevitable; but to preserve peace im-

perialist aggression must be halted. The combined forces of the socialist countries, the developing countries and the labour and peace movements in the capitalist countries are strong enough to achieve this, provided they act in a resolute way. (p35)

Opposition to British imperialism and active support of national-liberation struggles represent the second aspect of the Communist Party's internationalism. On this it has a proud record, and in 1970 Idris Cox could rightly declare:

The Communist Party was the first and only political party in Britain which has always recognised that the struggle of British workers is inseparable from the struggle for national liberation, from the necessity of united action of all those oppressed and exploited by British imperialism.[1]

Only the most significant landmarks of the CPGB's anti-imperialist record can be given here[2] – the "Hands off China" campaigns in 1925-26 to prevent British military intervention against Chinese patriots fighting for independence; the support of the movement against British rule in India until independence was won in 1947; the post-war support given to national-liberation movements of peoples belonging to the British Empire; and the solidarity campaigns with Vietnam until the Vietnamese won their complete independence by defeating the most powerful imperialism in the world. This anti-imperialist record is naturally reflected in the Communist Party programmes, the pre-war as well as the post-war ones, all of which include the anti-imperialist demands corresponding to the then prevailing situation.

A crucial demand which did not and could not arise before the war is the demand for British national independence from the USA. Why this became particularly important in the post-war period was explained in the 1951 *BRS*:

For the first time in its history, our country has lost its independence and freedom of action in its foreign, economic and military policy to a foreign power – the United States of America. (p10)

In demanding national independence for Britain, the *BRS* had not suddenly become chauvinistic and nationalistic. It merely applied to an unprecedented situation the standard Communist thesis that when a nation is enslaved by a stronger imperialist power, the fight for its independence is part and parcel of the international class struggle. It was certainly ironic that it was now Britain, which had formerly ruled over one quarter of the world, which was now threatened with enslavement, but the irony of the situation did not make it any less urgent to wage the struggle. It was especially important to reject new fashionable theories about the allegedly obsolete character of demands for national sovereignty. As the 1951 *BRS* puts it, these theories "seek to justify enslavement to American imperialism or aggression against other nations" (p11), even if they are sincerely held by people who think that they have a left, internationalist flavour. For, as the *BRS* went on to say:

> Real international co-operation can be based only on the sovereign freedom and equal rights of all nations, great and small. Because of this, the cause of Britain's national independence is bound up with ensuring that all nations in the present Empire also enjoy full national rights and independence. (ibid)

An important part of the Communist Party's anti-imperialist policies is its stand on the Irish question, not only because Ireland was Britain's first colony, but because Marx's view that British workers would never be really free until Ireland itself was free has remained valid ever since it was first put forward in the middle of the last century. This was implicitly recognised by all Communist Party programmes, from *FSB* which demanded "the withdrawal of all British forces and administrative personnel from Northern Ireland" (p44) and friendly relations with an independent Ireland, to the 1978 *BRS* which also demanded the eventual withdrawal of British troops but put forward a number of practical measures to precede and prepare such a step:

> [Britain] should ensure a democratic solution in Northern Ireland, based on the implementation of a Bill of Rights, the end of all repressive measures, the withdrawal of British troops to barracks, and financial and other measures to begin to tackle the appalling problems of poverty and unemployment. These steps would create conditions in which sectarian strife could be ended and British troops withdrawn completely. (p43)

And like *FSB* before it, the 1978 *BRS* envisaged "a new relationship of co-operation between the peoples of Ireland and Britain". (ibid)

Two controversial features of the Communist Party's Irish policy must be briefly mentioned. The first one concerns its attitude to the Provisional IRA. Understandably, this is not discussed in any of the programmes since it applies to the methods of struggle of the Irish people whereas the Communist Party feels qualified to speak of the road of advance in Britain. All the same, the condemnation of IRA tactics as counter-productive might not have been out of place,[3] even if couched in the most general terms. For example, successive editions of the *BRS* could have included the attack on individual terrorism which is found in the 1939 *DP* (a programme committed to violent revolution!):

> The Communist Party opposes all individual violence and ter-
> rorist acts on the part of the oppressed, under whatever provo-
> cation, and declares that liberation can never be won by such
> methods, but only by the mass struggle of the workers. (p38)

The other feature is the suggestion, put forward in the 1978 *BRS* for the
first time, that British troops should be confined to barracks, pending their
ultimate withdrawal after a political settlement. The reason which the party
leadership gave for this approach – not in the *BRS* incidentally – is that the
situation in Ireland is unique in that the country is deeply divided, unlike
other British colonies where the national movement was united and quite
ready to take over from the imperialists. As a result of the sectarian divisions in Ireland, the departure of British troops before a political settlement
had guaranteed a minimum degree of stability in the area could have tragic
consequences. The opponents of this approach reject it as patronising towards the Irish people inasmuch as they are thought incapable of running
their own affairs without the British. They also complain that, wittingly or
unwittingly, the Communist Party's stand brings grist to the mill of those
who claim that the role of British troops in Northern Ireland is to keep the
peace.

Lastly, a few words about the Communist Party's links with the international Communist movement and its attitude to the socialist countries,
although this aspect receives too brief a statement in the *BRS*, as has already
been regretfully pointed out.

When the CPGB was founded in 1920, it became part of a highly centralised organisation, the Communist International (Comintern or CI for short),
also known as the Third International. At that time all-Communists expected that a revolution in most European countries would soon follow the 1917
Russian Revolution, so that the activities of all CPs had to be co ordinated.
In all its pre-war programmes, the CPGB proudly proclaimed the fact that
it was a member of the Communist International. Thus, the 1929 manifesto
opened in the following way:

> Chapter 1
>
> The Communist Party
>
> The Communist Party is the party of the working class, in fun-
> damental opposition to all other parties. It is part of the Com-
> munist International, the international workers' party, leading
> the workers and oppressed toilers of the world, the vast major-
> ity, in the world revolution. (p5)

The same pride was expressed at the end of *FSB*, in the appeal to join the

Communist Party:

> ...the only Party that can lead the working class to victory - the
> Party of Lenin, of Stalin, and of Dimitrov – the International
> Party of the working class. (p48)

The 1939 *DP* went one stage better and in the second section of its ninth
chapter, "Marxism and Reformism in the International Labour Movement,"
it gave a brief historical account of the foundation of the First and Second
Internationals and explained why a new International, the Third International, had to be set up in 1919. It then went on to declare:

> The Communist International has made repeated overtures to
> the Labour and Socialist International ... for an international
> united front to make possible common action of the interna-
> tional working class. Under the influence of the reformist
> leaders of the Labour Party, all these offers have so far been
> rejected. This rejection is largely responsible for the successes
> achieved by fascism in a number of countries in recent years
> and for the extension of fascist war. (pp57-58)

This statement contained part of the truth, but not the whole truth. For it
was not only the LSI's rejection of unity with the Communists which was
responsible for the victory of fascism in Germany, but also the Comintern's
own sectarianism during the "Class against Class" period.

What is, however, beyond doubt is that, despite its mistakes, the Communist International's role was, on the whole, very positive. It helped its
member parties, the CPGB in particular, to adopt a class approach in politics, to fight on two fronts – against right-wing opportunism and left wing
dogmatism – and in the end, to stand on their own feet and work out their
policies independently. For the highest tribute which can be paid to the Comintern was that the time soon came when it outlived its usefulness as a
guiding centre. By 1935, its Executive Committee had already decided to
give all CPs a considerable degree of autonomy, partly because they were
all mature enough not to require day-to-day guidance, and partly because
the situation in each country was so vastly different from that in other countries. In 1943, the Comintern dissolved itself and each CP ceased to have any
formal links with other CPs.

However, that was not the end of international solidarity among Communists. During the Cold War period, roughly from 1946 to 1956, solidarity took the form, and had to take the form, of siding resolutely with what
was called "the camp of peace and socialism, headed by the USSR", against
"the camp of imperialism and war, headed by the USA". For example, the
1951-52 *BRS* denounced the anti-Soviet, anti-national-liberation policies of

"American big business ... backed and assisted by Britain" (p5) and contrasted this with the attitude of the peace camp:

> The peace camp... works for world peace and international co-operation and a Peace Pact between the Great Powers, the freedom and equal rights of all nations, the banning of the atom bomb, and the reduction of armaments. (ibid)

That was the kind of policy which Britain was urged to support.

With the Cold War having become a thing of the past, and also as a result of de-Stalinisation (which involved among other things the rejection of the view that the Soviet Union was a model and that the CPSU enjoyed a privileged position as the leading force in the movement), international solidarity took on yet another form. It became the purely voluntary support which each CP gives to other CPs, a support which involves popularising and praising their achievements, putting forward constructive, comradely criticisms of their shortcomings and deciding on a number of joint actions such as the fight for peace and disarmament. The 1978 *BRS* has this to say concerning one of the main distinctive features of the Communist Party, viz:

> ...it needs to have close relations with the Communist movement in other countries, based on the independence and equality of each Communist Party in a world movement which is making history on a global scale. Such international solidarity is vital not only in the immediate struggles but also for the achievement and building of socialism. (p26)

This raises the final issue to be discussed in this chapter, attitude to the socialist countries. As already mentioned earlier, the first thing to be said about these countries is that they represent an issue which cannot be evaded by British (or any other) Communists. For years, capitalist propaganda has been waging a virulent ideological campaign against the Soviet Union and other socialist states in order to discourage people from seeing socialist solutions out of the crisis. "Socialism = Gulag" is the simple, crude equation which is repeated ad nauseam by the government, other political parties and the media. Moreover, when we speak of the socialist society which we want to build in Britain, those who listen to us are bound to ask the inevitable question, "What about Russia? Poland? and so on..."

It is tempting perhaps to suggest that since these countries are an "embarrassment" and are always used against us, we should simply wash our hands of them or even go so far as to say that what we want for Britain is the exact opposite of what has been tried in the USSR and elsewhere. But this apparently easy way out is deeply mistaken. First, because our socialism may be highly original and specifically British, but it is still socialism, and as such, is bound to have something in common with the socialist experience of other countries Secondly, because, far from being an "embarrassment," the socialist countries are a great asset. We are the only political party which can speak of socialism, not as an unknown quantity, but as a reality, a reality which, in the words of the 1978 *BRS*, shows "socialism's great potential for human development".

Ah, but it works at a price, our opponents reply. In answering this, we point out, first, that capitalist propaganda deliberately distorts reality when it depicts life in the socialist countries as hell on earth, committing in this respect sins of omission as well as commission. Secondly, we, for our part, do not go to the other extreme and pretend that everything in the USSR, in Eastern Europe, in Cuba and in Vietnam is just heavenly perfect. There is no human society without problems and contradictions, and the socialist countries are no exception.

Our lucid approach to the socialist countries helps us to be aware of their limitations, and above all, to understand why such limitations still exist. They exist because the majority of the countries concerned had to start from a much lower level of development than ours in Britain, either economically, or politically, or culturally. They exist because the socialist countries are not and cannot be cushioned off against the worst effects of the crisis in the capitalist world; in particular, they have to spend much more on defence than they would like to, and this is bound to slow down advance in other areas. Lastly, one of their most serious limitations is that the bureaucratic methods of a recent past have not been completely wiped out. Such a radical break with long-established practices takes time and requires determination. We are confident that the socialist countries will be increasingly successful in extending and improving democracy, all the more so if we in the West can bring to power progressive governments which are not hysterically obsessed with the idea that everything must be done (from sabotage to war threats) in order to weaken the "Reds."

Our confidence is not a form of wishful thinking, but it takes into account both the nature of socialism (which needs democracy) and what has already been achieved. For example, we welcome all the measures taken in recent years to achieve even greater popular involvement in running the country as well as the many campaigns against red tape and bureaucracy. The new methods of work introduced by Gorbachev and the 27th congress of the CPSU are particularly significant in this respect.

The last point which need to be made on this issue is that our solidarity with the socialist countries is part and parcel of the class struggle which is taking place on an international scale. The arms race is a source of enormous profits for a tiny handful of already immensely rich capitalists. Worse still, the arms race is the last desperate attempt of the part of the Western ruling classes to halt the advance towards socialism and national liberation. Rather than lose their imperialist privileges, they are prepared to plunge the whole world into the nightmare of a nuclear war. "Better dead than red" is their motto, except that they will take great care to ensure that it is the common people who die, not their precious selves.

The preservation of peace has become the paramount duty of mankind today. It cannot be achieved without the socialist countries, whose record shows that they are earnestly trying to avert a third world war. Unlike the imperialists, they have nothing to gain from war. They need peace. So do we all.

NOTES

1 Idris Cox, "50 years Against Imperialism," in *Marxism Today* (October 1970), p.297.

2 For further details see Idris Cox's article (pp297-305) mentioned in note 2 above.

3 For details about the Irish Communists' attitude about the Provisional IRA, see James Stewart, "The Situation and Struggle in Northern Ireland," in *Marxism Today* (August 1975), p242. The whole article (pp232-44) is worth reading for a Marxist-Leninist treatment of the Irish problem.

5

The Party

The first Communist programme ever to be published anywhere in the world was the 1848 work of Marx and Engels generally known as the *Communist Manifesto*, but whose full title was *Manifesto of the Communist Party*. In this most famous Marxist classic, the point was made that the aims of Communism had to be presented through a party. That crucial point was also made in all Communist Party programmes. Again and again they stressed that the working class needed its own organised political party in order to provide guidance to the labour and progressive movement in its struggle to build a new society. What kind of party? What kind of guidance? What kind of relationship to other working-class parties and organisations? These are the three issues we shall briefly examine.

If there is one thing about which non-Communists and Communists are almost sure to agree, it is the fact that the Communist Party is different from all other parties. Its distinctiveness is seen as its greatest weakness by its enemies and yet as its greatest strength by its followers. How did the various Communist Party programmes present the party's distinctive features?

In the 1929 manifesto, the CPGB is described as "the deadly enemy of capitalism and capitalist parties", and the first of its aims is '(the leadership of the working class in the overthrow of capitalism" (p5). It would be a great pity if the somewhat intransigent language made us forget for one minute that, sectarian as the 1929 manifesto may have been, it expressed all the same a fundamental truth about the Communist Party when it gave as its first distinctive feature its "deadly" opposition to capitalism. Modern Communists can be proud of being the heirs of people who expressed such sentiments. They can equally be proud of the lucidity and courage which led to the following statements:

> Three parties – Tory, Liberal and Labour- appeal to you in the name of the "NATION." One Party – the Communist Party – appeals to you in the name of the working class. No Party can serve two masters. No Party can serve the "Nation" so long as the nation is divided into two warring classes – one which owns the wealth and one which produces the wealth and does not own it. No Party can serve the robbers and the robbed at the same time. To speak of the "Nation" when it is thus divided is camouflage to hide their support of the robbers because the great majority of the nation belongs to the class which is robbed. The Communist Party is thus the only party of the workers, the oppressed. (p7)

Quite a few criticisms may be levelled at his part of the manifesto, eg. the lumping together of Labour with the Tories and the Liberals or the failure to declare that since the great majority in Britain are working people, only the party of the working class can speak of the nation – without inverted commas. But such justified criticisms should not obscure the manifesto's great merit, viz its lack of hypocrisy, its refusal to pretend that it speaks for everybody (the robbers as well as the robbed), its uncompromising alignment with the working class. By all means, let us be critical of our past mistakes, but in the same spirit as Lenin when he criticised the youthful impatience of Britain's early Communists. The way in which he managed to combine criticism with admiration when he wrote about them in 1920 deserves to be quoted, if only as a refreshing antidote to the patronising and contemptuous nonsense with which our modern revisionists regale us when they pour scorn on their "primitive" opponents. After quoting a fiery letter from William Gallacher, Lenin wrote:

> In my opinion his letter excellently expresses the temper and point of view of the young Communists... This temper is very gratifying and valuable ... People who can give expression to this temper of the masses ... must be prized and every assistance given to them.

Then – and then only did Lenin add:

> At the same time we must openly and frankly tell them that temper alone is not sufficienct to lead the masses in the great revolutionary struggle...[1]

In *FSB* the last chapter is devoted to "The Communist Party." Its very existence as a party "steeled in struggle and capable of leading the workers to victory" (p46) is one of the key factors which makes the socialist revolution possible. The Communist Party is described as "the vanguard" of the working class, first, because it is made up of the most class-conscious elements of the working class, and secondly, because it knows "how to struggle", having as its guide "the revolutionary science of Karl Marx and Friedrich Engels, developed and enriched both in theory and practice by Lenin and Stalin" (ibid). Because the CP is the party of the working class, it "draws on itself the bitter enmity of the capitalists" (p47), but one of the great advantages of capitalist hatred is that it "weeds out any weaklings in the ranks of the revolutionary party" (ibid). *FSB* ends with an appeal to "every class-conscious worker to join the Communist Party without delay" (p48).

In the 1939 *DP*, there are numerous references to the need for a Communist Party and to its main characteristics. The first mention occurs at the end of the second chapter, in the section entitled "Marxism." After saying that Marx and Engels made socialism into a science, the *DP* adds that:

> ...in order to vanquish the old world and create a new, class less society, the working class must have its own working class party which Marx and Engels called the Communist Party. (p16)

The second mention occurs in the fourth section of Chapter 4, "The leadership of the revolution." The *DP* states that both in the struggle for conquering power and for maintaining power, victory requires:

> ...as its indispensable condition the leadership of a single centralised political Party of the working class, based on the principles of Marxism, and solely devoted to the aim of the victory of the working class and the establishment of socialism; the Communist Party. (p40)

Finally, the Party is mentioned twice in Chapter 9 which deals with "The Road to Power." After giving a short historical account of the struggle between Marxism and reformism in the labour movement, the section entitled "The Communist Party" describes the CPGB as the party of Marxism and adds that its chief characteristics are its working-class roots, its discipline, its dedication, its socialist aims, and its untiring work "for the unity and solidarity of all workers" (p61). A little further down, in the section entitled "Marxist theory and the Party," the programme stresses that one of the original features of the CP is the "training of its members in the principles of Marx, Engels, Lenin and Stalin" (p61).

One must note that political education, both the education of party members and the education of the broad masses by means of socialist propaganda, has always played a key role in the Communist Party's work, and furthermore, that it has never been looked upon as an academic exercise, but a guide to action. As the 1939 *DP* points out, its purpose is "to strengthen and knit the Party for the fulfilment of its tasks" (ibid). Moreover, again as pointed out by the *DP*, a good grounding in Marxism helps to overcome the two main dangers in a Communist's practical work, opportunism and sectarianism.

In the first versions of the *BRS* (1951, 1952 and 1958), it is the final section which is devoted to the Party, under the title of either "the Communist Party and the Way Forward" (1951-52) or "The Communist Party and the Labour Movement" (1958). The first one reasserts an important idea first put forward by Marx and Engels in the 1848 *Manifesto*, viz that "the Communist Party has no separate interests from the rest of the working class (p22). (Although not using these very words, all subsequent programmes make the same point.) It also reasserts the party's aim of "unity of all sections of the people" (ibid) in order to build socialism, its nature as a vanguard, and finally, the fact that "its policy and programme is based on the impregnable foundation of Marxist theory" (ibid).

In the 1958 *BRS*, the section on the Party is longer. The new points that it makes are first, a reference to democratic centralism (this was mentioned in the 1939 *DP* but not in *FSB*), secondly, a mention of the daily paper, the *Daily Worker*, and thirdly a demand for the removal of bans and proscriptions against Communists. Although as in all programmes, both those which came before it and after it, the fact that "the British working class needs the Communist Party" (p28) is forcefully made, there is a greater recognition of the role that other sections of the labour movement have to play, among them the Labour Party, the trade unions and the co-operatives. We shall return to this point further down in this chapter.

In the 1968 *BRS*, "The Role of the Communist Party" is discussed at some length in the second chapter of the programme which is called "The Communist Party and the Labour Movement." The most important novelties- in terms of presentation or in terms of content- are the assertion that the Party "combines campaigning of immediate issues with the fight for political power and socialism" (p23), that "its industrial branches provide an important means for mobilising and exerting the political strength of the working class" (ibid), and that an increase in its strength and influence would decisively affect "the outcome of the struggle between left and right in the labour movement" (ibid). The role of the *Morning Star* as the successor of the *Daily Worker* is described as being "unique" because the paper, being the only one in Britain to be "free of the press lords" (p25), can provide "a platform for every section of the anti-monopoly struggle"(ibid).

In the 1978 version of the *BRS*, the section devoted to the Party is part of the second chapter, which is called "The Forces for Change in Britain." It is a long section (pp25-29) of which the main features are as follows. First, there is a list, presented almost in a tabular form, of the party's five essential characteristics, viz that it is "based on Marxism-Leninism" (p25); that it is "firmly rooted in the working class, because of its leading role in society, and especially in the industrial working class" (p26); that it is "a democratic party" (ibid); and also a centralised one, capable of fighting "as a disciplined and united collective once policy is decided" (ibid); and finally, that it has "close relations with the Communist movement in other countries" (ibid).

Secondly, the party programme frankly discusses the steps which must be taken in order to improve the CPGB and enable it to become a "mass party". It explains that this last phrase does not only mean "a party with a bigger membership" (ibid), but one whose members are "drawn from and involved in every section and area of our society" (ibid).

Thirdly, in view of the revisionist attacks on the *Morning Star*, what the 1978 programme has to say on the subject deserves to be quoted in full:

> The only national daily newspaper which is co-operatively owned and free of control by the press lords is the *Morning Star*. Maintained in existence, with its predecessor the *Daily Worker*, since 1930, by the tireless support of its readers, it acts as a forum for the labour and progressive movement, advocating left unity and putting the case for socialism. Helping to build the broad democratic alliance, it forges links between the labour movement, other social forces, and wide sections of the British people. Its role is crucial, and all on the left should support it and help to increase its circulation. (p29)

All this is as valid today as it was when it was first written.

From the brief account given above, it is clear that the features which are common to all the programmes concern the party's basic nature and the kind of guidance it is expected to provide, whereas the most important difference (leaving aside differences in formulation or in emphasis) concerns the issue of whether the CP's role is one of exclusive leadership or not. Let us deal with the common features first.

The most striking of these features may appear at first sight to be such a truism that its significance might be overlooked – it is the fact that all the programmes have emphatically asserted that the British working class needs a Communist party. For the programme of a political party to make such a point is not as obvious as it might seem, for in the case of other parties, their existence is taken for granted. Their defenders naturally defend the virtues they are supposed to possess, but they do not feel that they have to show the historic necessity of founding such a party. Yet, this is just the claim which the Communist Party repeatedly makes.

It does not simply offer a policy, but an organisation which can fight for it. When it calls upon individuals to join its ranks, it asks them to become part of a collective fighting body which has a community of will and purpose. Hence the long-standing emphasis on the need for party members to be among the most dedicated, the most militant and the most class-conscious elements of the working people.

The other characteristics of the Communist Party which are mentioned in all its programmes are its social nature (working-class roots, yet open to all those who fight monopoly capital), the scientific basis of its policies (the Marxist-Leninist method), and its internationalist outlook. These characteristics determine the kind of guidance, practical and theoretical, which has been consistently demanded by the Communist Party. The practical guidance involves initiating, co-ordinating or supporting struggles on all issues affecting the working people; working in broad organisations, in which respect for majority decisions does not preclude the Communists' right and duty to put forward their own point of view as patiently and as cogently as possible; and mobilising the industrial strength of the working class, as the CPGB did so successfully in the course of the 1972 and 1974 miners' strikes. Theoretical guidance involves untiring, continuous and systematic socialist propaganda, oral and written, and presupposes a high level of political understanding among party members.

We now come to the party's leading role, an issue about which there is a substantial difference between the early and the more recent programmes. The difference can best be illustrated by considering the article before the expression "leading role": it was, implicitly or explicitly, the leading role up to the 1951-52 *BRS*, and it became a leading role from 1958 onwards. This issue is naturally linked to the Communist Party's attitude to the Labour Party.

In the 1929 manifesto, as we know, the Labour Party was described as the "third capitalist party", but as until then it had been customary for the CPGB to support Labour candidates in national and local elections, the authors of the manifesto felt the need to include a whole section entitled

"Our changed attitude to the Labour Party." They explained the new Communist approach by saying that the 1924 Labour government and the LP's betrayal of the General Strike had shown that it was no longer possible to put working-class pressure on the Labour Party. It had in fact become "a completely disciplined capitalist party" (p9). As only the Communist Party stood for a policy of "class against class", it was the only one the workers should trust, now and in the future. Moreover, since the reformist leaders had "transformed the Labour Party from a federal organisation to a single party with a capitalist programme" (ibid), the 1929 manifesto did not include the demand for the CPGB's affiliation to the LP.

By the time *FSB* was produced in 1935, the sectarian approach of the "Class against class" period had been given up, but as *FSB* just preceded the adoption by the CPGB of the Popular Front strategy, it did not express any positive comments about the Labour Party and it did not mention affiliation. Instead, it assumed that eventually the Labour Party would disappear, its best members having joined the only legitimate party of the working class. This assumption, which was maintained even at the time of the Popular Front, was based on the belief that social-democracy was, at best, an aberration which experience would eradicate, or at worst, a form of betrayal which again experience would finally expose.

The social roots of reformism, as distinct from its ideological roots, were either ignored or thought to have no bearing on the issue. In other words, the authors of *FSB* – and with them the party as a whole – believed that there was no room for more than one working-class party either before the revolution, or still less, after it. That different social experiences and situations led to different social experiences and situations led to different ideological attitudes – an elementary point for historical materialists – and that for a long time to come workers might retain reformist or semi-reformist ideas without necessarily being class traitors were points which do not seem to have occurred to the CPGB in the 1930s.

In this respect, the last pre-war programme, although being more realistic than its predecessor, continued to look forward to the establishment in Britain of a "single united political party of the working class", and in order to avoid any misunderstanding, it added immediately that such a party would be "based on the principles of Marxism" (p59). On the other hand, what represented an undoubted advance was that the Popular Front experience had brought the issue of affiliation back to the fore. In the 1939 *DP* it was mentioned twice, first, in the chapter dealing with "the Road to Power," and secondly, in the preamble to the immediate programme in the last chapter.

In the first one, the authors of the *DP* said that:

> The building of the Communist Party and the fight for its affiliation to the Labour Party is the indispensable task of the labour movement. (p57)

And a little further down they added that the CPGB sought affiliation:

> ...in order to strengthen the united action of the working class against capitalism and in order to assist and further the political development of the labour movement. (p59)

Both formulations show that affiliation was sought, not as a temporary tactical measure, but for principled strategic reasons. It was linked to the building of the Communist Party and its success was regarded as a great contribution to the raising of the political consciousness of the whole working-class movement. What is especially significant is that this approach, which is realistically suited to the unique conditions prevailing in Britain, was considered by the *DP* to be a key factor in the road to power, ie that its importance transcended the immediate present. We have here in embryo a specifically *British Road to Socialism* (even though the phrase was not used) rather than the mere repetition of a general truth, viz that a revolutionary party is needed for the victory of the socialist revolution. Not that the *DP* denied that this was the case. Its merit was that it applied this principle to British conditions and realised that the British revolutionary party had first to become part of the existing mass organisation of the British working class in order successfully to exercise its leading role.

The second reference to affiliation in the 1939 *DP* was the statement made in the preamble to "The immediate programme" according to which the election of a progressive Labour government would be brought about by:

> ...the unity of the working class through the affiliation of the Communist Party to the Labour Party, and joint action by the united working class with other sections ... (p63)

The stress on unity was, of course, part and parcel of the Popular Front strategy, but the actual experience of the period when this strategy was fought for by CPs was that the reformist leaders were still reluctant to cooperate with the Communists. This was particularly true in Britain, but the collapse of the Popular Front coalition in neighbouring France was an additional reminder that the achievement of working-class unity had by no means become a certainty. It is therefore not surprising that, despite its broad-mindedness, the 1939 *DP* contained some pretty strong attacks on reformism, described at one stage as "the deadliest enemy of the labour movement, a weapon of the ruling class against the working-class revolution" (p50).

The same attack on reformism was to find its way in the first version of the *BRS*, but this time it was directed against the practice of the 1945-51 Labour governments. In the 1951 version, the reformist leaders were accused of paving the way for the Tories, but in 1952, after such a prediction had been proved correct by the Tory electoral victory at the 1951 General Election, the authors of the *BRS* could write that it was the failure of the Labour government to bring about "basic social change" which had made possible "the establishment of a Tory government which is ... bringing new difficulties to Britain".(p3)

In both versions, we find that millions were urged to fight against both the Tories and the right-wing Labour leaders, but apart from this appeal to individual Socialists, the *BRS* did not examine the forms which working class unity might take. For example, it had nothing to say about affiliation. The impression conveyed by the document is that, at the height of the cold war, the CPGB regarded itself as being the leading socialist force, not so much because of a dogmatic decree on its part, but because that was what the facts were showing.

It is part of the tragedy of the cold-war period that the facts were right and that the CPGB was the only organised force which was fighting for socialism in Britain. Like all political parties at the time, it may have allowed itself to become hard-line and intransigent, but at least, in its 1951 and 1952 programmes, it was passionately describing working-class unity as "the vital need" (1951 *BRS*, p16 ,1952 *BRS*, p13).

When the 1958 *BRS* came out, the Cold War had been buried for some time, but the Communist movement had just gone through another traumatic experience – the "agonising reappraisal" initiated by the 20th congress of the CPSU. New questions had arisen as well as new answers to old questions. Among the latter, one was the reassessment of the Communist Party's role. In order to appreciate how the 1958 *BRS* broke new ground on this issue, it is useful to refer to JR Campbell's article in the 22 September 1956 issue of *World News* in which he outlined the main changes which the commission set up to revise the party programme was proposing to make.

After saying that the section on "The Communist Party and the way forward" must seek to close the gap "between the daily activity of our Party and the prospects outlined in the programme", he went on to say that the new *BRS*:

> ...must show the difference between unity of action embracing Labour and Communist workers, on immediate questions; unity of the Labour Party and the Communist Party in common actions; and, on the other hand, an unprincipled "unity at any price," involving the sinking of Communist principles and the liquidation or near-liquidation of the Communist Party ... It is precisely at this moment, when the reformists are trying to drag the movement backwards, to the acceptance of a refurbished programme of social reform under capitalism, that our Party has to fight most vigorously to create a genuine socialist outlook in the Labour movement.[2]

The last section of the 1958 *BRS* fully corresponds to Campbell's wishes. On the one hand, it shows the distinctive character of the Communist Party and it stresses that it is irreplaceable, but on the other hand, it is no less emphatic that:

> There is no conflict between the Communist Party and the Socialist members of the Labour Party, trade unions or Co-operative movement. (p29)

The common denominator is spelt out, viz:

> We are all working to end capitalism and win socialism. We all

realise that it can only be achieved by the industrial, social and political struggles of the working class. (ibid)

Thus, the stress on unity and the absence of sectarianism are not achieved by diluting the party's commitment to revolutionary Marxism and to socialism, but are in fact the direct result of such a principled commitment. In 1958, as throughout its entire history until the 1980s, the CPGB was capable of being broad and flexible in its approach and its tactics because it was inflexible about the fundamentals of its theory and outlook.

On the issue of a single working-class party in Britain, the 1958 *BRS* still thought it a desirable aim, but it used the conditional tense to describe the likelihood of its happening:

> The removal of the bans and proscriptions directed against the Communist Party is the first step in restoring unity to the movement. This could lead to further steps towards unity including the possibilities of affiliation, and eventually of a single working class party based on Marxism when the majority of the movement has been won for the Marxist outlook. (p29)

We shall argue in a minute that the prospect of a single party is unrealistic, but we must praise the 1958 *BRS* for being the only programme apart from the 1939 *DP* to mention affiliation, another crucial issue to which we shall presently return.

A striking novelty in the 1968 *BRS* is the assertion, never made before in a CPGB programme, that:

> Contrary to the ideas spread by some Labour leaders it is not the aim of the Communist Party to undermine, weaken or split the Labour Party. (p24)

This does not mean that the fight against reformism is toned down in any way, for the programme goes on to say that:

> When the Labour Party rejects reformism, moves onto attack on capitalism, ends the bans and proscriptions against the left, it will ensure itself a vital role in the building of socialism. (ibid)

Further down in the chapter dealing with the socialist society which will be built in Britain, the *BRS* declares that the LP and the CP "would be the political organisations of the working class, primarily responsible for the success of the building of socialism" (p56). There is no suggestion that the Labour Party will have to become Marxist before it can play a useful role. Acceptance of the Marxist standpoint," says the programme, "can only come through personal conviction, and the fruit of experience, discussion, argument and study" (ibid). The CPGB's affiliation to the LP is not mentioned, but on the other hand, the prospect of a "single united Marxist party" is put forward for the distant future, ie "only when and if the majority of Labour Party members come to accept Marxist ideas" (ibid).

In this writer's view, this last prospect is somewhat unrealistic, because it is based on the assumption that in the course of fighting for socialism and in the process of building it, the majority of the politically conscious working class will necessarily accept the whole of Marxism.

What is more likely is that an increasing number will do so, whilst quite a few others will not go beyond giving their support to socialist policies. That would undoubtedly constitute a great achievement, but Marxism means more than that. It involves, among other things, a strictly scientific approach to politics, a dialectical understanding of the relationship between the present and the future, and a distinctive organisational structure for the party of the working class.

The 1968 BRS also shows that the growth of the Communist Party and the victory of the left inside the Labour Party are not opposed to each other, but are complementary. It is not at the expense of the LP that the CP will become stronger, but as part of a process of the common growth of the labour movement as a whole.

As workers increasingly take part in mass struggles, all sections of the movement will benefit, the working-class political parties as well as the trade unions, the co-operatives and the many organisations set up to achieve clearly defined objectives, such as women's liberation, racial equality, protection of the environment, and so on.

The 1978 BRS reasserts the CP's claim to give the labour movement "coherence and vision, and to exercise democratic leadership" (p28) and stresses once more that its object is not:

> ...to replace the Labour Party as a federal party of the working class, but rather to strengthen its original federal nature...

adding that:

> ...a much more influential Communist Party [is] crucial to the future of the Labour Party itself ... (ibid)

What the BRS looks forward to is that as the united struggle grows

> ...new opportunities will open up for still more developed forms of Labour-Communist unity, including in the electoral field, and with the possibility of future affiliation to the Labour Party. (ibid)

126

Whilst welcoming the reference to affiliation, one must regret that it is not included as one of the priorities which the left as a whole should be fighting for. Affiliation of the Communist Party to the Labour Party is vitally important to both parties. For the Communist Party, it would help to remove one of the biggest obstacles preventing its growth, viz the understandable fear on the part of many workers that supporting Communists would split the anti-Tory opposition. Thanks to the federal nature of the LP, such fears would be groundless once the CP became a constituent part of a broad organisation.

For the Labour Party, the affiliation of an organised body of militant socialists, with a long record of struggle, experience and dedication behind them, would prevent it from losing its socialist aims and its socialist conscience. It must be stressed, however, that what the Labour Party needs is not thousands of Communist individuals, but the Communist Party as a party. For it is as a party, and only as a party, that it can fulfil the role of democratic leadership to which it aspires and which the whole movement urgently requires.

The above pages have endeavoured to show that the "party" which the modern revisionists want is the negation of everything which has inspired and sustained generations of Communists. It is also the negation of the best traditions of the British labour movement.

NOTES

1   Lenin, *'Left-wing' Communism*, chapter 9.
2   JR Campbell, *"The British Road to Socialism,"* in *World News* (22 September 1956), p612.

6

Conclusion

A conclusion is often an author's way of imposing his/her views on the readers by taking leave of them with a few neat phrases that dispense with further thought and analysis. This is the first reason for not offering a conclusion at the end of this book.

A conclusion can also be a patronising way of bringing out the obvious for fear that readers might be too dense to see it for themselves. In the present case, it would simply amount to restating what successive Communist Party programmes have said and to recapitulating the analysis of the issues involved. This is a second reason for not offering a conclusion at the end of his book.

A conclusion may unwittingly suggest that the matter is now closed and that the book one has just read is the definitive answer to all the problems which it raises. Nothing could be more opposed to Marxism, which is a living doctrine, always in the making, and a guide to action. This is a third reason for not offering a conclusion at the end of this book.

Lenin's question, "What is to be done?", which could well serve as a sub-title for the present book, has been given many answers by British Communists over the years. The same question is destined to have many more answers, to be worked out collectively both in theory and in practice. This is a fourth and most important reason for not offering a conclusion at the end of this book.

7

Postscript

A continuous guiding thread has run through these successive Party programmes analysed by Max Adereth. They have all aimed to mobilise, in opposition to big business, an alliance of that huge majority of the British people whose interests are threatened by it. Many sections of them are initially far from seeing their future as bound up with ending capitalism. But none of them can defend itself against its main enemy without the support of the working class, and the working class cannot emancipate itself from capitalist exploitation except by socialism.

In Britain, the working class, broadly defined, is overwhelmingly the largest force within the alliance, the most homogeneous in its interests and, as a result of its long history of struggle within capitalism, much the best organised and most experienced. So while the winning of allies, however temporary or conditional, is important, the struggle to unite the working class must never be subordinated to it. Yet downgrading the role of the working class was the core of the revisionists' conception of the broad democratic alliance. Not surprisingly, they were happy to define the working class as manual workers alone, since they were falling in number.

In the sphere of politics, mobilisation means creating, by struggles which change the balance of forces, the self-confidence that comes from imposing real material changes on the enemy, and the consciousness of the escalating steps that must yet be taken if political power above all, state power – is to be wrested from big business and placed firmly in the hands of the working class and its allies. For only with state power can working people bring under their own ownership and democratic control the decisive means of production, the source of all economic power.

But the general strategy of mobilisation always takes on a particular form, conditioned by place and time. Today it is one for Britain in the 1990s, with its historically specific external and internal class relations, its present stage of state-monopoly capitalism, its possibilities of wealth enhanced by the scientific and technological revolution, but restricted by the continuing history of imperialism. And all this within the world context of a changing balance of forces of imperialism and those for human progress and socialism.

If the maximum possible forces are to be mobilised for defending past gains and a socialist future, we need to analyse precisely what those forces can be, and what issues and forms of struggle can fulfill their potential.

Max Adereth's own narrative, to judge from internal evidence, was completed toward the end of 1986, long before the collapse of socialism in the Soviet Union. But his last article, written in early 1989[1] identifies democracy as the very core of socialism, in a way very similar to that expressed by the CPB in its 1992 Congress Resolution "The Collapse of Socialism in the Soviet Union". He wrote:

> the very meaning of socialism is being critically re-examined, not in order to give it up as a regrettable error, but in order to strengthen and fully release its democratic potential. It is now strikingly evident that socialism needs democracy in order to succeed and go forward. At the same time [as he quotes from Gorbachev. RB], 'democratisation is real when it rests on a solid basis of social ownership and absence of exploitation'.

These 1989 remarks suggest an advance on his view three years earlier, expressed in the present book. At that time, his legitimate critique of Eurocommunism led him to attack "the view that existing socialist countries were undemocratic". But in modifying his own view as new evidence came forward he was neither alone nor unMarxist.

However, he did not live to see the Draft of the 1989 *British Road to Socialism*, though he took part in the early discussions which led to it. It is to this that we now turn.

Changes in the context since the end of 1986

Two changes in the *BRS* were made after Max Adereth's narrative finishes. The first – the new edition of 1989 – arose from the re-establishment of the Communist Party in April 1988 on the basis of the existing Constitution and the existing *BRS* of 1977, with an undertaking that the latter should be revised at a Special *BRS* congress in November 1989. The second, that of Chapter One "The World Situation", was called for by the Congress of 1991. It was necessary to examine the new world conditions of the struggle for socialism in Britain brought about by the collapse of socialism in Eastern

Europe and the Soviet Union.

The changes introduced by the 1989 *BRS* flowed from the decade of struggle against the revisionism, which led to the collapse of the CPGB.

One result of that decade was the almost complete absence of Marxist education within the CPGB and of Marxist analysis of contemporary Britain. Hence the new *BRS* had for the time being to take on some of the tasks which had in happier days been performed by the Party's journals and its inner-party education. The CPB, small at its re-establishment and with many of its members scattered, did not have either material or human means to sustain the width of propaganda, theoretical and educational material possessed by the old CPGB.

Moreover, the latter's own material since the late 1970s, especially *Marxism Today*, was totally unusable. It is true that the struggle against revisionism had created a deep need for discussion of theoretical questions, and the lack of practical activity in the CPGB's latter days had left energy for it, which *Communist Campaign Review* between 1986 and 1988 sought to marry. But once the Party was re-established, its energies were focussed on renewing practical communist leadership.

The *BRS* itself had therefore to be capable of providing material for study. It became longer. This applies even more to the "Revised Chapter on the World Situation", where Communists everywhere in the world had to rethink their strategy within a totally new balance of world forces. This scientific analysis is fundamental to a Marxist party, but a shorter version is needed for wider dissemination.

What was new in the 1989 BRS?

(1) The class content of a "broad popular alliance" or "broad democratic alliance" is re-emphasised in two respects.[2] First, restoration of the words "anti-monopoly" makes clear that it is the giant capitalist transnational companies and banks who are the main enemy of the British people. This was intended by the 1977 Congress, but its formal omission from the programme provided the gap through which revisionism marched to impose its classless version of the alliance.[3]

Second, the leading role that the working class must achieve in that alliance is re-emphasised as essential if the alliance is to stay firmly on the road toward socialism. These two steps consolidated the victory won in a decade of ideological struggle against revisionism. The need to re-establish the Communist Party on this basis has been amply justified by the path which the revisionists have now completed with the dissolution of the CPGB, and its replacement by the Democratic Left, which no longer regards itself as a political party. It has carried to the logical end the view of the group around *Marxism Today* that the working class was just one – and not the most important at that – of many "social forces". With no roots in the working class, the Democratic Left has abandoned any serious connection with Marxism.

(2) The second development is a deeper analysis of the working class consistent with the "broad" definition inherited from 1977, which embraces all those who work for a wage or salary and are not in any controlling position. This definition was not accepted in 1986 by Max Adereth, as evidenced in his article in the first issue of *Communist Campaign Review*. His own view was one which has been widely used in the European Communist movement, and in some Soviet and East European practice. For example, both Soviet and GDR statistics distinguished "workers" from "employees" and, in the Soviet case, also from "intelligentsia".

Only the main points at issue can find space here. A fuller justification for the broad definition has been presented by the present writer elsewhere.[4] This in fact provoked no discussion, nor were any amendments tabled on this issue at the 1989 Congress. However, in looser discussions terms such as "middle class" are not uncommonly – and quite inaccurately – used to refer to some salaried workers, even though their incomes and economic insecurity are today converging toward those of skilled manual workers. The foundation of the *BRS* definition is that the class position of a group is determined by its relation to the means of production (production relations), and not by the nature of the work it does (Marx's "concrete labour" ie its place as a productive force). That the latter cannot be a satisfactory criterion is exemplified by the case that agricultural workers and peasants alike perform the same concrete labour, but peasants own their tools and their own product. It is this they sell, not their labour power.

Two quite different concepts have been used to defend a narrow definition. The first is that only those are workers who create surplus value. Even on this definition, the class would have to include all members of what Marx called "the associated labourer in production" and not just those who in the most direct way transform material nature. Marx was entirely clear that this "labourer" included storekeepers, technicians, designers and so on.

In our time, the ranks of the associated labourer extend much further than in Marx's. He also included among "productive" workers school teachers who worked for a private school owner, (and how many of our teachers are now moving toward this position!) because what mattered was not whether they produced material things, but whether they produced surplus value for their employer.

For Marx, the narrow working class also included all wage earners "who continue the process of production in the sphere of circulation". Hence all who work for wages in shops etc, are workers in the narrow sense. The fashionable "predominance of a service economy" has sometimes been uncritically accepted by some who would at the same time vehemently object to putting railworkers or lorry drivers outside the ranks of the working class.

Finally, state employees (outside nationalised industries) do not produce surplus value because they produce nothing saleable. But they perform surplus labour which is appropriated by their state employer, and their exploitation helps to keep down the costs to the capitalists of running the state.

Of course, the above cannot fully cover all the subtle, and changing, boundaries of real life. Trade union and political practice demands that position of foremen, junior managers, technicians, cultural workers etc, is constantly reviewed. But practice demands the same for manual workers, for example those of an imperialist country, or those who work for "a monopoly that has plenty of gravy to share".

The general acceptance of the broad definition had probably less to do with the theoretical argument outlined above, than with the experience that white-collar workers joined trade unions, became involved in the traditional forms of struggle, and began to develop a working-class ideology.

The *BRS* treatment, therefore, stresses the common – and generally converging position of all who sell their labour power. But it also distinguishes a section of the working class concentrated in large enterprises (ie large firms, usually with many workplaces). These workers have an objective position in class relations and in the class struggle more generally in which they need to and can develop higher levels of consciousness and organisation.

(3) Extra-parliamentary struggle is emphasised as primary in its unity with parliamentary struggle. Attention is drawn to the richness of forms and organisations that the people would develop in the course of the struggle for state power. But speculation as to the precise form of the transition is resisted, as this depends upon the balance of forces which will exist at the time. Emphasis is placed on the need to develop now a fight for democratisation in all the organs of state, and especially in the armed forces and the police.

(4) Much more precise and richer answers are given to the question of stages in the mobilisation of forces for advance to socialism in a Britain marked by imperialist decay – that is, to the question of an intermediate strategy linking the immediate struggle to the ultimate goal. The left in the labour movement, and most consistently the Communist Party, had developed from the late 1960s an Alternative Strategy for Britain, a reply to the Tory slogan "There is no alternative". In the versions adopted by the TUC and the Labour Party, this tended to be limited to economic policy only (AES), and its implementation bureaucratically by a labour government. There was no sense that radical political changes were at stake, which could never be carried through unless supported by a powerful mass movement and a much more united working class. Not surprisingly, when Labour lost the election in 1979, this programme went into limbo. In the CPGB likewise, though an Alternative Economic and Political Strategy was spelled out by the 1983 Congress, it significantly appeared in the "Tasks Facing the Trade Unions" and not in the general "Political Resolution". In any case, it was ignored by a leadership which had in fact already abandoned all alternatives based on class struggle.

(5) New evidence on the absence of democracy in communist parties which had held state power led, as in 1956, to criticism of democratic centralism itself. But the majority view stressed two thing. First, that in any body bent on action, unity in carrying out decisions required centralism. But decisions would be the best possible, leading to willing support in action, only if they resulted from democratic discussion. Second the unity and discipline of a party would be self-imposed by its members to the extent that the shared Marxist outlook and approach to problems was mastered at every level.

(6) A new section was entailed by the growing pressure of ecological problems and world poverty. its essence is the need to move:

> toward an overall system of production in which waste must either be recycled or used as the starting point for other processes. This system is incompatible with the continued existence of an unplanned capitalism dominated by transnationals and the drive for maximum private profit. But experience of socialist countries shows that environmental protection will demand constant vigilance, public awareness and democratic involvement.

The 1992 Congress revision of Chapter 1:
The World Situation

The 41st National Congress of November 1991 took place amid the final stages of the collapse of socialism in eastern Europe, and four months after the abortive coup of August 1991 in the USSR, with the subsequent rise of Yeltsin. An entirely new balance of forces in the world made obsolete the chapter of the 1989 *BRS* which dealt with the world situation, including the socialist countries. To avoid premature judgments in a fluid situation, the congress decided to reconvene itself in November 1992. It then did so on the basis of a Draft Resolution "assessing the collapse of the Soviet Union", and a Draft for a Revised Chapter 1 of the *BRS*: The World Situation."

The first resolution met the Party's demand that it "express a point of view" on the collapse, but it was not a part of the Party's programme. The new chapter of the *BRS*, on the other hand, must be a part, because it estimates the drastically changed world framework within which a *British Road to Socialism* must now be fought for.

On socialism, the revised chapter said what was universally agreed, that:
> Only if the main means of production are collectively owned by those whose labour sets them in motion, and only if the people fully exercise their rights of ownership and have full control of their own future can the creative initiative of tens of millions be mobilised...

The only model of socialism that is capable of winning the allegiance of the working class is that which starts from Lenin's conception:

'Comrades, working people. Remember that now you yourselves are at the helm of state! No-one will help you if you yourselves do not unite and take into your hands all the affairs of state ... Socialism cannot be decreed from above. Its spirit rejects the mechanical bureaucratic approach; living, creative socialism is the product of the masses themselves'.

Before 1917, the whole world was under capitalist domination. By their scientific analysis of the laws of development of society, and of capitalist society in particular, Marxists had given the working class confidence that it could win political power and emancipate itself through social ownership and popular control. This analysis has rightly been summarised in the programmes of all Communist parties.

This is more than ever necessary today, when few workers under the age of 50 have had the systematic education which used to be the hallmark of the CPGB. Initially at least, a large part of the responsibility for making good falls upon the BRS.

Moreover, an objective situation has emerged which is entirely unprecedented in the lives of all communists – and the lives of all capitalists too. After the collapse of the European Exchange Rate Mechanism (ERM) in 1993, the capitalists' triumphalism looks premature and immature. For communists, concepts which had too often been taken on trust, insufficiently examined and hardened into dogma, were rightly questioned. There was and is considerable disorientation and lack of confidence even in key concepts themselves.

In that context, it is important not to conceal the Marxist method which is being used, but to show it openly, even if the skeleton sticks out through the flesh. That is why the past development of the world capitalist system is shown to develop through contradictions within it between the social character of production and the private capitalist nature of property ownership, between its consequences in the struggle between the working class and the capitalist class, and the struggle between sections of the latter leading to imperialist war and creating the conditions for socialist revolution.

To that complex system of contradictions, 1917 added another that between capitalism and socialism.

It was this contradiction that for the whole of our lives – and particularly for those lives spent entirely under the shadow of the Cold War – dominated the whole complex. Above all, even after Germany and Japan came back into the struggle for their "place in the sun", inter-imperialist tensions were largely subordinated to the need for political and military unity against the socialist countries. Moreover, in that unity the predominating strength of the United States guaranteed her first place.

If that contradiction between imperialist states is removed, the tensions between the imperialist powers predominate over their new unity.

This new emphasis prompted a more general examination of developments within imperialism which had in fact been taking place for some time, but had been masked from us for a number of reasons which there is no space to examine here. It may be too that British communists, rightly conscious of their colonial and neo-colonial history, has failed to notice Lenin's warning that imperialism did not confine its drive for domination to agrarian or backward countries. At any rate, we had not noticed the direction which overseas investment by imperialist metropolises had taken since the mid-70s.

So when the conflict between capitalism and the socialist countries was no longer there, two initial reactions were common. The first was a revival of an old Maoist slogan that the contradiction between imperialism and the Third World would now be centre stage. The second, linked closely with the first, was that there would be a New World Order of inter-imperialist unity in which the United States would reclaim the full hegemony it had enjoyed immediately after WWII.

The revised chapter shows by careful analysis of the facts that the second underestimates the growing severity of inter-imperialist conflict as Japan and Germany grew faster than the US. In a more limited arena, the present breakdown of the ERM evidences similar conflicts between European imperialist powers sharpened by a world slump.

Looking more carefully than before at the detailed facts, the *BRS* also shows that while the poverty of the Third World has its roots in the continuing depredations of imperialism, the very large majority of capitalist profits, through direct investment of TNCs and through trade and usury, arises in relations among the developed capitalist countries themselves, and to a smaller extent in those with Newly Industrialising Countries. It follows that the class struggle between the working class of these countries and the imperialists, and the rivalry between the imperialists themselves, form the central contradictions of the world capitalist system today and for the near future. In order to fight out this rivalry, the ruling class of each imperialist country seeks to increase economic resources at the expense of the working class and to meet its resistance with further moves towards political and ideological reaction.

It would be arrogant to claim that this is some final assessment. Continuing discussion at a national level and international level is required.

But one thing is certain. The severity of these conflicts, aggravated further by a cyclical crisis of overproduction, expose world capitalism as the very opposite of a smooth engine for growth and welfare. In the fight for their future within capitalism and their emancipation from it, working people everywhere need the Marxist analysis, and the leadership based on it, that Communist parties provide.

Ron Bellamy

NOTES

1 Max Adereth, "A Consistent Class Policy", *Communist Review,* no 3
   Spring 1989.
2 Ron Bellamy, "Revisionism and the 1977 *BRS.*" Ditto.
3 Tony Chater, "A Strategy for Advance." Ditto
4 Ron Bellamy, "The Definition of the Working Class" *Communist Review*
   nos 4, 5, 6

Bibliography

CP Programmes
Class against Class, General Election Programme of the CPGB (May 1929)
For Soviet Britain (February 1935)
Draft Programme submitted to the 16th Party Congress (August 1939)
The British Road to Socialism (January 1951)
The British Road to Socialism (April 1952)
The British Road to Socialism (February 1958)
The British Road to Socialism (October 1968)
The British Road to Socialism (March 1978)
The British Road to Socialism (January 1989, with revised chapter on world situation 1991)

Histories of the CPGB
Tom Bell, *The British Communist Party: A Short History* (Lawrence and Wishart, 1937)
Noreen Branson, *History of the CPGB: 1927-41* (Lawrence and Wishart, 1985)
James Klugmann, *History of the CPGB*
    Volume 1: Formation and Early Years (Lawrence and Wishart, 1968)
    Volume 2: The General Strike 1925-26 (Lawrence and Wishart, 1969)
Henry Pelling, *The British Communist Party: A Historical Profile* (Adam & Charles Black, 1958)
Rene Salles, *Structure, Implantation et Influence du Parti Communiste de Grande Bretagne dans une perspective historique* (PhD thesis submitted in 1978, published by Universite de Lille, 1981)

Other useful histories
M Adereth, *The French Communist Party: A Critical History, 1920-84* (Manchester University Press, 1984)
Alien Hutt, *British Trade Unionism: A Short History, 1880-1961* (Lawrence and Wishart, 1962, 1975)
The Post-war History of the British Working Class (EP Publishing Ltd, 1974)
AL Morton, *Socialism in Britain* (Lawrence and Wishart, 1963)
AL Morton & G Tate *The British Labour Movement* (Lawrence and Wishart, 1956)
AI Sobolev et al, *Outline History of the Communist international* (Moscow, 1971)

Biographies and autobiographies
William Gallacher, *Revolt on the Clyde* (Lawrence and Wishart, 1936, 1978)
    The Rolling of the Thunder (Lawrence and Wishart, 1947)
    Rise Like Lions (Lawrence and Wishart, 1951)
    Last Memoirs (Lawrence and Wishart, 1966)
John Mahon, *Harry Pollitt: A Biography* (Lawrence and Wishart, 1976)
Harry Pollitt, *Serving My Time* (Lawrence and Wishart, 1940)

To the above one must add the countless books and pamphlets put out by the CPGB to explain its policies (the most important of which are mentioned in the course of this study) and the following newspapers and periodicals:

Dailies
Daily Worker (1930-66)
Morning Star (1966-)

Weeklies
Inprecorr (Comintern journal-English edition) (1921-37)
World News and Views (1937-53)
World News (1954-62)
Focus (1982-85)

Fortnightlies
Comment (1963-82)

Monthlies

Labour Monthly (1921-81)
Communist Review (1921-27 and 1946-53)
Marxism Today (1957-1991)

Quarterlies

The Modern Quarterly (1938-39 and 1945-53)
The Marxist Quarterly (1954-57)
Communist Campaign Review (Communist Campaign Group) (1986-88)
Communist Review (Communist Party of Britain) (1988-)

Index

Milton Keynes UK
Ingram Content Group UK Ltd.
UKHW020413311024
450335UK00003B/42